INSCAPE
GOD AT THE HEART OF MATTER

by

GEORGE A. MALONEY, S.J.

DIMENSION BOOKS
DENVILLE, NEW JERSEY

248
Ma I

Imprimi Potest: Rev. Eamon Taylor, S.J.
Provincial of the New York Province
May 10, 1978

—Dedication—

*To Andrea Federoff who has taught
me that not all contemplatives
are to be found in monasteries.*

ACKNOWLEDGEMENTS

Sincere thanks to Sister Joseph Agnes of theSisters of Charity of Halifax for reading and typing this manuscript. Grateful acknowledgement is made to the following publishers: Darton, Longman & Todd, Ltd., and Doubleday & Company, Inc., N.Y. for excerpts from *The Jerusalem Bible,* copyright 1966 by Darton, Longman & Todd, Ltd., and Doubleday and Company, Inc. All scriptural texts are from *The Jerusalem Bible* unless otherwise noted.

TABLE OF CONTENTS

INTRODUCTION............................... 5

1. A NEW AGE—A NEW VISION............. 13

2. THE UNCREATED ENERGIES OF GOD.... 26

3. EYES TO SEE GOD EVERYWHERE........ 49

4. GOD AND MAN AT WORK................ 74

5. MARRIAGE AND CONTEMPLATION......101

6. TO BE EUCHARIST..................... 126

7. COME ASIDE AND REST AWHILE....... 151

8. IN HIS PRESENCE...................... 173

FOOTNOTES................................. 200

INTRODUCTION

In the ancient days, when the first quiver of speech came to my lips, I ascended the holy mountain and spoke unto God, saying, "Master, I am thy slave. Thy hidden will is my law and I shall obey thee for ever more."

But God made no answer, and like a mighty tempest passed away.

And after a thousand years I ascended the holy mountain and again spoke unto God, saying, "Creator, I am thy creation. Out of clay hast thou fashioned me and to thee I owe mine all."

And God made no answer, but like a thousand swift wings passed away.

And after a thousand years I climbed the holy mountain and spoke unto God again, saying, "Father, I am thy son. In pity and love thou hast given me birth, and through love and worship I shall inherit thy kingdom."

And God made no answer, and like the mist that veils the distant hills he passed away.

And after a thousand years I climbed the sacred mountain and again spoke unto God, saying, "My God, my aim and my fulfillment; I am thy yesterday and thou art my tomorrow. I am thy root in the earth and thou art my flower in the sky, and together we grow before the face of the sun."

Then God leaned over me, and in my ears whispered words of sweetness, and even as the sea that enfoldeth a brook that runneth down to her, he enfolded me.

And when I descended to the valleys and the plains God was there also.[1]

This is a book about man and God growing together. Man descends to the valleys and plains of his mind and finds God there in all of his human experiences, stored up in his consciousness and unconscious. He discovers God in the valleys and plains of this earth, in the market place of his daily labors, in the sacredness of his family life at home, in the joys and sufferings that each day brings him.

But God is to be discovered "inside" of matter, through His dynamic energies of life, as He and man cooperate to transform the materiality of this world into a realized, spiritual presence of God within the human community. Yet how few human beings, even Christians, can find God in matter with any consistent ease and habitual attitude? God is present. Are we present to God? In the words of Gerard Manley Hopkins, S.J., "These things, these things were here and but the beholder wanting."[2]

A MASCULINE CIVILIZATION

The poet Tagore, in the decade before World War II, voiced the problem which is still very much our own contemporary problem.

Civilization is almost exclusively masculine, a civilization of power in which woman has been thrust aside in the shade. Therefore, it has lost its balance and is moving by hopping from war to war. Its motive forces are the forces of destruction and its ceremonials are carried through by an appalling number of human sacrifices. This one-sided civilization is crashing along a series of catastrophes at a tremendous speed because of its one-sidedness. And at last the time has arrived when woman must step in and impart her life rhythm to the reckless movement of power.[3]

Modern psychology describes the integrated human person as a harmonious blending of two psychic principles. The *animus* is the intelligible principle of analysis, which gives birth to critical reflection, to control and calculation. The *anima* is defined as the principle of relationships, of communion and unity.[4] Man and woman make contact with God in a "feminine" relationship, an attitude of reverence and waiting for God to take the initiative to reveal Himself. If He is always present and, therefore, always revealing Himself to us and if we are not always *seeing* Him and *listening* to Him in His revealed Word, shining *diaphanously* (to use Teilhard de Chardin's favorite expression) through the material world, then it is because we have not developed the contemplative side of our human nature.

I have used the phrase *inscape,* coined by G. M. Hopkins, to suggest this contemplative attitude of Christians going inside of matter to find there the uncreated energies of the immanent Trinity, loving and serving us unto our healing and happiness. For Hopkins, *inscape* is the "outward reflection of the inner nature of a thing." He defined it in 1886 as "the individually-distinctive beauty" of each creature.[5] It is the "thisness" or the "selfing" that makes every animate or inanimate creature a distinctive individual. For St. Maximus the Confessor of the 6th century, it is God's gift to the pure of heart to see God's *Logos* in each creature and to adore that Holy Presence by a working with God's Mind to reconcile all things to God.

This is a book about our contemplating such a loving, energetic God working in all things. It calls for us to work together with God's loving energies. Using insights from the Greek Fathers concerning contemplation and a theology of *grace* as the "uncreated energies" of God in all of creation, I have sought to bring together an incarnational spirituality as the basis of a contemplative prayer for moderns living in a busy, exciting world.

AN EXHAUSTED SPIRITUALITY

In our exploding universe of today, the traditional views, presented by Western Christianity and based largely on an exhausted scholastic philosophy and theology, concerning man, God and the material world, no longer seem adequate. A spiritual vision is needed to offset the Augustinian Platonism that has accounted for an un-Christian separation of nature and supernature and a heavy dichotomizing between man's body and soul, matter and spirit, the secular and the sacred.

Our heavy rationalistic framework that has served to present Christianity to the West is in need of a complementary vision. Such a "new" vision is really not old. It is found in the Old and New Testaments. It is grounded more in perceptual, intuitive knowledge. It is an openness to God as mystery in which man meets the transcendent God in a reverential awe and wonderment. Yet God's transcendence cannot separate Him from man. Man is rooted in God as in his Ground of being. Yet that Ground, because God is so completely transcendent, is also rooted *immanently* within man. As Jesus Christ is the meeting of divinity and humanity with neither of them inseparable, and yet each of them distinct, so also man, in all of his materiality and finite humanness, is not to be separated from God living within him, even though God is not man and man not God.

The uncreated energies of God touch man. Man's created energies touch God. The divine and the human co-penetrate each other. They are inseparable from each other, yet each order possesses its unique "otherness" and distinction.

A spirituality is needed that will break away from the heavy objectivization of body and soul and nature and supernature that has given Western Christian spirituality an unhealthy attitude toward the human body, the material things of this world, sexuality and marriage; in general, toward any serious involvement in the human situation.

The Greek Fathers, in a process theology rooted in the Hesed covenantual, condescending, loving activities of God in all things, offer us a basic corrective in their mystical theology of contemplating God as uncreated energies. God is absolute Transcendence in His essence. But for us this God does not exist in our experience. The only God we can come to *know* and experience is the God who relates to us as He in His holiness and humility wishes to share His life with us. God "goes forth" toward us in His uncreated energies. As related to us and His creatures, God is *grace*. He is loving energies in His Self-giving to us. God is working equally in *nature* as well as in *supernature*. The whole material world is saturated with God's loving, activating energies.

ALL IS SACRED

Can anything of the secular world keep out God's sacred and holy, energizing presence? We cannot *escape* from a material world to find God only in *sacred* places and occupations. We need to *inscape,* right into the heart of matter, and find the heart of God, creating out of love this or that unique creature. Matter, work in the world, our contemporary history, sex and marriage must be seen positively as permeated with God's loving, creative power. The material world must be a help now for us to find God there and adore Him. The active and contemplative lives are a single life of contemplating God within us and without us. Our work now becomes worshipful prayer as we put on the mind of God's Logos, Jesus Christ, to co-work in a *synergy* with God's energies to fulfill the universe.

I have tried in the following chapters to trace the lines of a vision of the unity of all things in Christ Jesus. Treated in detail are the topics of the uncreated energies of God, the sophianic Logos mysticism of the Greek Fathers, God and man at work, marriage and contemplation, the call to be Eucharist to the world, the need of deep, centering prayer as the basis of a synthesis of the active and contemplative aspects of our lives and, finally, contemplation as a state of praying always by living consciously, through God's infusion, in His loving presence in all events of our daily lives.

God is calling all of us to become contemplatives, not in spite of the world, not by running away from an evolving, material world that at times perhaps groans in travail louder than it whispers songs of glory to God, but precisely by running into the world. There is God. It is for us, with pure hearts that have been emptied of all selfishness, to open our inner eyes to see Him there. We adore Him in awesome worship. We also adore Him as we give ourselves to build the earth into the Body of Christ. Only the Christian contemplative in the future will survive, both as a Christian and an authentic human being, for only such a person will be growing daily in love of God and loving service of his neighbor. The rest of human beings will be "dead-souls," ravaged by the specter of Meaninglessness in their lives.

> Plum-purple was the west; but spikes of light
> Spear'd open lustrous gashes, crimson-white . . .
> And through their parting lids there came and went
> Keen glimpses of the inner firmament.[6]

1

A New Age—A New Vision

The human race has entered into a new age. We presently are too close to the launching of it to be able to know what is really happening in our modern world and to see where it will lead us. At any rate, we find ourselves caught in a strong tension similar to an adolescent who gropes for meaningfulness in the new-founded powers that slowly emerge from within him and explode confusedly around him.

We are tensioned between a feeling of pessimism, even fear, and an optimism that excites us with fanciful dreams of a world of infinite richness. Our new age is symbolized by our entrance into space exploration, by the launching of the Soviet *Sputnik I* on October 4, 1957 and our American *Explorer, I,* launched on January 31, 1958. We have walked with Neil Armstrong around Tranquillity Base on the moon. Each day we learn more about the red plains and the deep chasms of Mars.

Through satellite communication we are in immediate touch not only with planet Earth and its Earth people, but also with other planets as well. In a way, our universe is shrinking in the sense of all parts of it becoming more and more "present" to modern man. Yet in another way, we stand in a frightened isolation "against" that unknown world, exploding before us into mysteries that we cannot handle with our limited, human knowledge.

One way to cope with such multiple richness and apparent meaninglessness is to retreat into *ourselves*. We can build physical and psychological walls around us and, within the narrow confines of self-centered consumerism, drugs and alcohol, sports, cults, new and old religions that tend toward building a ghetto, we can live in "splendid isolation" from the rest of the world.

A NEW RELIGIOUS OUTLOOK

The traditional views presented by Western Christianity and based largely on an exhausted scholastic philosophy and theology, concerning man, God and the material world, no longer seem adequate. In the late 1960's a religious counter-culture began. Indian gurus flocked to America and introduced the younger generation to the treasures of Yoga and Transcendental Meditation. Zen monasteries popped up in suburbia and Jesus communes developed away from the cities.

Western organized religions that tended toward teachings and dogmas, hierarchical structures of authority and liturgical ritualism, found a need to revitalize themselves. The faithful were in search of transcendence and personal experiences with their God.

Through our hyper-activism and the depersonalization of our technological world, all of us cry out for a greater sense of personhood and individuation in our relationships, both with one another and with God. M.

Rokeach and E. Chesen have pointed out how conformity to external, religious forms and a rigid belief system can lead to immature and even detrimental psychical development.[1]

Jung, more than any other modern psychiatrist, has shown how some people use the institutional, dogmatic and ritual aspects of their religion as a defense against subjective, inner religious experience. Strongly does he advocate in his writings that the quest for religious experience is an integral and necessary part of the search for self.[2]

Our heavy rationalistic framework that has served to present Christianity to the West is in need of a complementary vision. Such a "new" vision is really not old. It is found in the Old and New Testament. It is grounded more in perceptual, intuitive knowledge. It is an openness to God as mystery in which man meets the transcendent God in a reverential awe and wonderment. It takes man's eyes away from himself as the exploiting center of the universe and focuses man's attention on a humble response to God's invitation to share His divine life.

Abraham J. Heschel captures this contrast between a heavily accentuated, rational approach and that of perceptual intuition:

> Most of our attention is given to the expedient, to that which is conducive to our advantage and which would enable us to exploit the resources of our planet . . . However, as we have seen, there is more than one aspect of nature that commands our attention. We go out to meet the world not only by way of expediency but also by way of wonder. In the first we accumulate information in order to dominate; in the second we deepen our appreciation in order to respond.[3]

BODY-SOUL PROBLEM

The way we perceive ourselves as human beings is the way we shall also relate to other human beings and to God. For centuries we have viewed man as an entity, existing all by himself. We have failed to see him as a person orientated toward others in body-soul-spirit relationships. Instead, through Platonism that became the principal carrier to express a Western Christianity, man was defined in terms of someone made up of a body and a rational soul.

Even though Plato himself strove to show the cohesion of body and soul in making man a oneness, a person, nevertheless, as C.A. Van Peursen shows,[4] Plato could not put them side by side on the same plane. For Plato, the soul is of a different order from the body. It is an entity that existed before it entered into the body. This coming together is conceived of as the result of a fall from a higher state of perfection.

In the 17th century, Descartes did more than any one thinker to create the impression of the body and soul as two distinct, objective entities. Although philosophically he strove to maintain the unity in man, he did oppose body and soul on the level of two entities of the spiritual and the material that mutually are distinct and separated from each other.

Such an objectivization of the body and the soul has left its heavy mark upon our Western Christian idea of death. In death, for the majority of Christians, it is believed that the body of the deceased is solely the cadaver that is put into the earth while the soul wafts off to an objective place called Heaven, Purgatory or Hell. At the final resurrection that soul will zero back into the cadaver and the individual will be resurrected from the dead.

A similar meditation is usually given of the soul of Jesus returning from its peregrinations around Limbo after three days to re-enter His mutilated body in the sepulcher. The result is the Risen Jesus passing through the tomb, much to the fearful amazement of the soldiers who were guarding the tomb.

BODY, SOUL, SPIRIT IN SCRIPTURE

In the Bible we are given a vision of man, not in philosophical terms, but of man in his relationships with fellow-men, with God and with the whole created world. Through modern biblical research, theologians like Karl Rahner, Paul Chauchard and many others[5] have sought to present man in terms of body, soul and spirit relationships, a view, such thinkers feel, as more consonant with the concept of man as presented by the writers of the Bible. St. Paul describes man in a process of becoming holy and blameless, "spirit, soul and body, for the coming of our Lord Jesus Christ" (1 Th 5:23).

The Old Testament uses the word *neshamah* to mean *breath* and *life* as found both in God and man.[6] "Then he breathed into his nostrils a breath of life, and thus man became a living being" (Gn 2:7). *Nephesh* is the more common term that refers to man's inner life-force, located in the blood. It is the source and *locus* of man's emotional and affective life. Man does not, in this sense, possess a life-giving soul, but becomes a living soul. Man has such an inner source of life affecting the whole of man's well-being. It is a rich concept that stresses the oneness in man. The Jewish mind could never separate man from his soul, but man would be considered as a "souled-being."

But the whole man is also a "bodied-being." Man is *enfleshed*. The Hebrew word for this is *basar* and the Greek word *soma* comes closest to translating it. Again, according to the Jewish mind, "body-ness" refers not to an objective entity of man but to the whole man in his state of transitoriness. Thus man in his *flesh* can long for God (Ps 63:1; 84:3). Flesh or body in man is the whole man considered as ephemeral, in contrast to God as spirit.[8]

Ruah is the more common Hebrew word used to express wind or spirit to indicate God's presence among men in His creative power. As *enfleshed,* man recognizes his creatureliness as gift from God. As *ruah* that God breathes into man, it is God's spirit or presence coming upon individuals and His people to restore them to new love relationships with Him (Cf.: Ez 36: 26-28). Thus in the Old Testament, man's body or *flesh* and his soul or spirit never imply a dualism, with two opposing, objectivized entities.

Flesh and spirit, therefore, describe different relationships of man to God, as a transient creature related to God as Creator, yet as a total being, formed and strengthened by God's loving presence or spirit.[8]

THE FLESH AND BODY IN THE NEW TESTAMENT

If we are to enter into a new vision of man in relationship to God, we must understand carefully the meaning of *flesh* and *body* as used in the New Testament, especially in the Pauline writings. As for the Old Testament writers and those of the New Testament, *body* (*soma* in Greek) does not refer to a part of man but points to the whole man in his potential for action in the temporal world. Man not only *has* a body but he *is* his body as he makes choices for his actions or accepts actions of others in obedience or disobedience to God.

St. Paul seeks to describe the total man, the flesh-substance, the whole man when he refers to man as "flesh" (sarx). The whole man is considered from the point of view of his external existence as opposed to any interiority. *Sarx* represents man in all his creaturehood in contrast to God. It is man, not only in his distance and difference from God, in his mortality and weakness, but also in his utter estrangement from God through sin. "Both Jew and pagan sinned and forfeited God's glory" (Rm 3:23).

All of humanity, both the Jew of the Law and the pagan guided by his conscience, has been tainted by sin, not only because of the first man's sin that brought death to all men (Rm 5:12), but also because sin has entered as a power subjugating man from without by using man's own physical flesh as the instrument for his estrangement from God. Sin wields an almost irresistible power over man, leading him away from God. One of its prime ways of enthralling man is through the material flesh. Man is sold into the power of sin (Rm 7:14). But sin and flesh are not the same thing (Rm 6: 12-19; 8:3; 12:1; 2 Co 4:11). But in his realism Paul shows the flesh as the seat of all passionate desires, set awry as long as man does not ascend and put on the "spirit of Christ." The *flesh* element is not sinful by its nature, but in fact it does open the door to sin through inordinate self-love.

CHRIST—THE REDEEMER

It is in the light, therefore, of the flesh-spirit antithesis that St. Paul highlights the saving, healing power of Jesus

Christ as Redeemer. Through the Incarnation, the Son of God broke through the barrier separating the realm of divinity and life from that of humanity and death, both physical and moral. Although personally sinless, Christ came "in a body as physical as any sinful body" (Rm 8:3). Christ took upon Himself our estrangement by becoming like us in all things, save sin. Although He was united intimately with the Father, Christ in His earthly existence was in some sense not fully one with His Father. By taking upon Himself our flesh (*sarx*) condition, He entered a humanity in a state of "unsalvation" which bore the sign of sin, namely, death (Rm 5:12).

Not only is man infected with sin and death, but the whole of creation has been touched by the power of sin. Man and the whole sub-human cosmos share the same fate of being subjected to sin and death and cannot reach fulfillment without the Savior.

> From the beginning till now the entire creation, as we know, has been groaning in one great act of giving birth; and not only creation, but all of us who possess the first-fruits of the Spirit, we too groan inwardly as we wait for our bodies to be set free (Rm 8: 22-23).

Yet God had mercy and sent His Son in the likeness of sinful flesh (Rm 8:3) to condemn sin in the flesh by dying on the cross and through His resurrection, to redeem the whole world, including all mankind, from sin. Jesus Christ passes gloriously from the state of flesh (*sarx*) according to St. Paul's teaching, to that of spirit (*pneuma*). As long as Jesus was confined, as we are, to His human flesh, He was not able to share His divine life with other human beings. But after His glorious resurrection, He, "the last Adam, became a spirit imparting life'' (1 Co 15:45).

St. John also affirms that before Jesus died, He could not yet send us His Spirit (Jn 7:37). Jesus Christ would effect the redemption of us and through us human beings also that of the whole universe by overcoming the flesh and leading it to spirit. Christ first experiences redemption within His own flesh-state. He conquers death by the transforming glory of His resurrection in which His carnal condition, that is, the state of estrangement from God, would be transformed into the fullness of Spirit of life of God. Just as His humanity was an integral part of His way of touching human beings, so now, by the resurrection of that same human body, the entire Jesus Christ can touch the bodiliness of all men and the whole universe to receive a new orientation to God. This reorientation would lead eventually to a full resurrection in the Spirit. The glorified bodiliness of Jesus becomes the source of the Spirit of eternal life.

MAN—THE DIVINE ICON

Holy Scripture and the early Fathers present man as unique among all of God's creatures. He alone has been made ''according to the image and likeness'' (Gn 1:26) of God. He stands over and against his Creator as a self-positing, free creature, as an *I*, capable of responding to God's invitation to become a sharer in His very own life (2 P 1:4).

God creates man's being in such a way that he knows that he is determined and conditioned by God, and in this fact is truly human.[9] Man's nature can never be static or finished. It is always in process of *becoming* more and

more, through man's free choices out of love for God, a
child of God. This is brought about by the Spirit of Jesus
(Rm 8:15; Ga 4:6). And man grows into this awareness or
consciousness in prayer as the Spirit reveals the infinite
love of the Father in Christ Jesus for this unique *I-Person.*

Man's nature can never be outside of God's loving activities. Grace, as God's primary presence in His uncreated
energies of love, bombards us from all sides, even from
within us by God's indwelling presence. God is loving us in
all creatures that enter into our lives. His *graceful* presence
is inside of each event, calling us to respond to His love.

THE UNVEILING OF GOD

If God, therefore, is so dynamically present to us, why
is it that we do not "see" Him everywhere? As has been
pointed out, our concept of ourselves as possessing objectivized entities of a body, soul and spirit, has led us to objectivize God also as an object existing outside of
ourselves, usually *above* us in some supernal region called
Heaven. As will be pointed out in the next chapter, our
conceiving of man's nature as distinct and separated from
the supernatural order has also blinded us to see God's loving presence in our human nature and in all of our
"natural" activities.[10] In a word, we conceive God in His
epiphany or His descent *upon* the earth, but we fail to see
His *diaphany,* to quote Pierre Teilhard de Chardin.[11]

Martin Heidegger furnishes us with insights for a new
vision of God and man in mutual relationships. For him,
God is a dynamic, energetic force, never static, but always
revealing Himself to us in the events of each day, in the
Sitz im Leben. Truth is an event, not an abstract concept.

It is an event of "non-concealment" or a "re-velation," a stripping away of the veil so that the fullness of Being may shine forth.[12]

But for the Christian of prayer, God never becomes fully revealed. He hides His full *Being,* His Godhead, but casts His light for the purpose of revealing human beings by calling them to a response as they experience God as the Ground of all beings. To *see* God in His revelation is to love ourselves and all other creatures by a created participation in the uncreated and all-powerful love of God.

GOD'S ENERGIES OF LOVE

It is especially in human relationships that God touches men and women in His most revealing, unveiling of His uncreated energies of love. "God is love and anyone who lives in love lives in God and God lives in him" (1 Jn 4:16). If God truly abides in us, He does so through all of His energizing love that becomes perfected as we love one another (1 Jn 4:8).

This does not mean merely in those deep, human love relationships with which God may gift us, but in all human encounters. God lies concealed, seeking to release His Spirit of love in each encounter, if we would only have eyes to see Him as the source of each human person's unique being. Teilhard de Chardin beautifully expresses this encountering of God in encountering the "other" in each other:

> . . . since my heart cannot reach your person except at the depths of all that is most individually and concretely personal in every 'other'—it is to the 'other' himself, and not

to some vague entity around him that my charity is addressed.[13]

Openness to God's presence in each human meeting characterizes the Christian who has first met the presence of God loving him in his solitary, interior prayer before the loving Father. He believes in God's presence, living and loving in the other person encountered. He hopes and trusts in God's love and thus does not aggressively judge or anticipate how God should reveal Himself in that meeting. Above all, the love of the Spirit allows him to give himself in delicate sensitivity to the other.

THE TRANSFIGURING CHRIST

As we break down the static elements in our concepts of God and the nature of ourselves and all other creatures that surround us, our prayer-life reveals a global presence of Jesus Christ as the activating Logos of the Father in all creatures and in all events. We see with interior eyes that have received the infusion of the Holy Spirit in faith, hope and love that the Risen Jesus Christ is inside of all that exists. God's energies bathe the whole universe with transforming love and yet those energies of God call out to us human beings to become "reconcilers" (2 Co 5:18) of the universe in order to fashion and mould the Body of Christ.

The material world is to be brought into spirit by our working with the Logos of God. Christ is evolving the universe, bringing all things into the fullness of God's plan (Col 1:20). Creation is not finished but is to be fulfilled by our creative response to the inside presence of Christ in all of matter. A new vision of Christ at the heart of matter is really an old vision, forgotten largely in the Western world.[14]

All of our actions, no matter how monotonous and seemingly "profane" and "natural", can contribute to make our world fulfilled. Such actions, rather than conceived of as simply *secular,* are points of meeting God's loving energies. The whole world becomes a sacred place in which to discover the humble God, serving His children. Like Jacob who wrestled with divine and human beings and prevailed (Gn 32:29), so we also meet God in our daily struggles to see inside of all matter and there find the face of God.

> To repeat: by virtue of the Creation and, still more, of the Incarnation, *nothing* here below is *profane* for those who know how to see. On the contrary, everything is sacred to those capable of distinguishing that portion of chosen being which is subject to the attraction of Christ in the process of consummation.[15]

Let us now turn to a development of the Eastern Fathers' doctrine of God's uncreated energies before we can present the other elements of a spirituality of finding God at the heart of matter.

2

The Uncreated Energies of God

Parents are still amazed and quite ready to dip into their pockets to purchase tickets again and again so that their children can see the intriguing movie: *Star Wars.* It is a science fiction with heavy spiritual symbolism of the eternal war between the forces of evil and good. But one reason, I suspect, for the most intriguing interest with which both children and grownups have viewed this movie is the person of Obi-Wan Kenobi played in an excellent manner by Alec Guinness. He appears as a "mystic" who is in touch with the *Force.* When he lets go and yields to this supernatural power that is everywhere exerting its good influence, great things happen. He is surrounded and covered by this Force or supernatural power. He can tune into it and share its great power to overcome the evil forces in the universe.

Edwin Scott Gaustad in his book, *Dissent in American Religion,* points out that a great religious dissent is taking place in America and it is moving in three new directions. "Dissenters opt for mystery, seek community, and embrace joy."[1] He points out that Americans are more and more seeking mysticism over a clinical rationality. The theology handed them for so long has become for them remote and lifeless and has been too much tied with an ecclesiasticism that has become impersonal and "correct" but does not speak to the needs of modern man.

On the positive side he points out that mysticism is awakening the powers of human creativity. Such a person who seeks mysticism is ever ready to be surprised by the hidden beauty that is in creation. Pointing out the low road that the quest for mysticism can take with all of its self-seeking, Gaustad describes the "high road" that the same quest can take.

> Deliberate acceptance of mysticism leads along the high road to humility. Man does not and will not know all, he cannot and need not control all. That high road also leads to the humane, to the needs of the person more than the dictates of the machine.[2]

The great danger with all religions is that after some time the masses of faithful lose true faith and settle down for man-made idols. Usually these false gods are fashioned out of a heavy excrustation of extrinsicism, formalities, doctrines and rituals which no longer serve to impart a true transcendent experience with the wild God of the burning bush. Human beings tend by their sinful natures to want to control the God they wish to adore. Religious persecutions always have a positive feature insofar as they purify the dross in a given religion and push the *Anawim* back to a direct encounter with their God of the desert through child-like faith and abandonment.

A TURN TOWARDS MYSTICISM

There can be no doubt, and it is surely more than a passing fad, that a great many people today are hungrily seeking a more direct encounter with God, an immediate experience of His reality in their daily lives. Too long they have lived a life that was "sacred" but all too divorced from their "secular" or ordinary life. The rapid speed of their lives today and the great mobility and change that they experience at their work and in their families call out for deeper, more conscious ways of coping with such changes.

Dr. Victor E. Frankl, the Austrian psychiatrist, has pointed out the growing *angst* or anxiety that fills the heart of modern man with a sense of meaninglessness.

> Effectively an ever-increasing number of our clients today suffer from a feeling of interior emptiness—which I have described as existential emptiness—a feeling of total absence of a meaning to existence.[3]

A heavy rationalistic theology has colored our prayer life and our daily perception of God and the world in which we live. Worn out by the Cartesian dichotomies that have separated thinking man from the natural world around him, modern man is eagerly looking for new alternatives that will allow him not only to grow religiously but to maintain his humanity in a sea of meaningless *bourgeoisie*. Dr. Louis Dupré analyzes the reasons for the loss of true transcendence in theology and in modern life today:

> From the sixteenth century on, however, reality became rapidly reduced to its objective, if not its physico-mathematical qualities. The one-sidedness of the new approach seriously impaired the mind's self-understanding and, for the same reason, its ability to conceive a genuine

transcendence. It even reduced our view of nature. What Heidegger writes about Descartes goes also for his successors: the world turned into a presence-at hand (*Vorhanden*), that is an exclusive object of manipulation, closed to contemplation.[4]

Many moderns are turning to the Far Eastern religions to learn the techniques that will allow them to enter into their inner selves and find the Divine within. Others are finding the authentic mystical tradition in Christianity down through the ages in both Eastern and Western Christian mystics. There is in the Byzantine Christian world a wealth of true mysticism that has not been known in the West, at least among the ordinary Christians. It is this fount of great wealth that I would like to explore in this book and open the reader to a new perception of God as uncreated energies of love in His constant relationships in all things with us. I would propose that this *apophatic* theology is the basis of an authentic mysticism that is not only available by God's designs to all Christians but I would even hazard that this is precisely why God created us "according to the image and likeness of God" (Gn 1:26) namely, that all of us might, both in this life and in the life to come, contemplate God as love in all things and love Him in return by our love and service toward others.

A KNOWING BY NOT KNOWING

We have used the word *apophatic* which is a key word among the Greek Fathers, rich in meaning and, I would like to think, in application and importance for us Western Christians. It normally is translated as the negation necessary to be added to any positive assertion about God's attributes. It is a humble confession of God's supreme transcendence that surpasses any human thought category. We can say God is this or that, but immediately we must say, no; He is *this* but never in the way we understand. God's uncreated energies can never be comprehended fully as expressed in human terms. What is said is true. Yet it is also false. God is so much more!

Yet this *apophatic* element is more than a mere negation in the area of linguistics. Its essential characteristic is positive. It is a *real* knowing. But it is a knowing on our part through a gifted experience in love. As we stand with Moses wrapt in trembling awe before the awesome God on the mountain top, God flashes His loving presence to us through the dark cloud of unknowing. We know God in a new way: by not knowing Him through our rational knowledge, but in an infused knowledge that God lovingly bestows upon His little children who cry out with hunger to look upon the face of their loving Father.

This is an immediate, experiential knowledge that God freely gives to us when He wishes. We can never cause this knowledge which would be the same as saying we can never force God by any of our actions to love us in a self-presence as Gift to us. True, God is prejudiced towards the humble, the poor in spirit, because He is truthful. He refuses to fill with Himself what is already filled with selfishness.

So when we hunger and thirst for His coming, through years of obedience and cooperation with His holy will, through intense and continued purification of our hearts of all self-centeredness, in a word, when we are disposed, then God, who has always been present, reveals Himself in a new way of knowing.

LUMINOUS DARKNESS

Chief among all the Eastern theologians who developed the positive aspect of apophatic mysticism was St. Gregory of Nyssa, the father of Christian mysticism. He influenced greatly the mystical theology of Pseudo-Dionysius whose writing with its mysticism of darkness influenced Western mystics, especially the Rhenish mystics of the 14th century like Meister Eckhart, John Tauler and Henry Suso and the Flemish mystic, Jan Ruysbroeck, all of whom had at least an indirect influence upon Spanish mysticism of the 16th century, chiefly upon St. John of the Cross and St. Teresa of Avila.

In St. Gregory of Nyssa's classical mystical treatise, *Life of Moses,* we have a full presentation of the individual Christian's movement toward full union with God, using the analogy of Moses' journey up Mount Sinai until he reaches God in an "understanding" that is only in darkness. The process is a stripping or a movement away from the sensible, the reasonable in order to meet God as invisible and incomprehensible in the darkening of man's powers. This St. Gregory well describes in his *Commentary on the Song of Songs:*

> Our initial withdrawal from wrong and erroneous ideas of God is a transition from darkness to light. Next comes a closer awareness of hidden things, and by this the soul is guided through sense phenomena to the world of the invisible. And this awareness is a kind of cloud, which overshadows all appearances, and slowly guides and accustoms the soul to look towards what is hidden. Next the soul makes progress through all these stages and goes on higher, and as she leaves behind all that human nature can

attain, she enters within the secret chamber of the divine knowledge, and here she is cut off on all sides by the divine darkness. Now she leaves outside all that can be grasped by sense or by reason, and the only thing left for her contemplation is the invisible and the incomprehensible.[5]

For the Greek mystics, the true theologians of the ear ly Church, God, the Incomprehensible One, is present and is experienced by the Christian. It is God's overwhelming transcendence that brings darkness to man's own reasoning powers. The emphasis is not on the incapacity of man, but rather on the overwhelming infinity of God, always present in His creation.

Presence and transcendence are one in apophatic theology. The contemplative, the one who is given *theognosis,* knowledge about God by God, directly in an experiential intuition, finds the paradox to be true, that as one comes closer to union with God, the more blinding God becomes. This is not a matter of the knowledge of God becoming more abstruse but of the nature of God itself becoming more present. This presence is brought about by the uncreated energies of God's loving activities surrounding us at all times in every event.

Pseudo-Dionysius took the mystical doctrine of St. Gregory of Nyssa and incorporated it into his famous classic, *Mystical Theology.* He teaches that the way in which we approach God and are united to Him is not the way of rational knowledge. It is the way of Inner Vision, though obscure to the normal, precise expectations of reason. The individual needs to be quiet and withdraw attention from sense experience and intellection.[6] As he silences his heart from all aggressiveness towards God and the world around him, the man of deep prayer begins to see how bound he is by shadow and darkness, by sense pleasures and false values.

BROKENNESS

Although God has been active as an energy-force in His creative Word throughout all of creation and we human beings can with our intellect understand something of God's presence as loving energy, yet the real presence of God as loving energy comes only in contemplative prayer when we move beyond our own controlled activity to enter into God's healing love. But the first stage of entering into contact with God's energizing love is for us to experience our own state of alienation away from Him. It is inside of ourselves that we must go, into the deeper reaches of our consciousness and unconscious, beyond our controlled knowledge that can so easily lead us to illusions and greater separation from God, into those areas of brokenness and meaninglessness and death and darkness.

It is when we have the courage to confront our dark side that Jesus Christ becomes an energizing force of love as He releases His Spirit so that we can surrender to our loving Father who dwells within and calls us evermore into our true nature as being one with His only begotten Son.

In the strange paradox of a living Christianity the contemplative enters into darkness and desperately cries out for the light of Christ. Caught in the death of a static self-centeredness, the individual begins to sense the uncreated energies of God's new life ready to burst in upon him if he only stretches out to possess those energies.

Prayer is born in such inner poverty of spirit. Man learns in his existential nothingness that only God is life, is energy, and all life must come from Him alone. He stretches out of his inner tomb for One to release him and bring him into new life. And in that yearning, he experiences a letting go of his own controlled existence as he knows his great need for the Other.

THE UNAPPROACHABLE ONE

In such brokenness the Christian knows that God is unreachable and unknowable. No matter how poor and empty we know ourselves to be and we do begin to feel God's infilling come upon us, still we also know that we will never in this earthly existence see Him face to face. Yahweh does show Himself to us as He did to Moses, but it is only His "back" that we see. "Then I will take my hand away and you shall see the back of me; but my face is not to be seen" (Ex 33: 23).

None of us can ever see God fully. "No one has ever seen God" (1 Jn 4: 12; Jn 1: 18; 6: 46). We would need to be also God, part of His essence, in order that we would know Him fully. Only a like nature could comprehend His nature. In spite of the revelation of the Father's love made to us by His Son, Jesus Christ, we shall never know Him fully. No matter how inflamed with His loving presence we have become both in this life and in the life to come, there will always be something *unfathomable* about God.

And that is why the Greek Fathers always insisted on the distinction between God's *essence* and His uncreated *energies.* This distinction is of paramount importance. On the one hand, it preserves the awesome transcendence of God that can never be totally possessed by finite creatures. In God's essence He is immutable, all perfect, unchanging.

We in no way can add anything to His perfections. God is completely independent of us.

Still, our Christian faith teaches us from Holy Scripture, God's revelation through His Word, that God in His holiness and humility wishes to share His life with us. If God is love (1 Jn 4:8), He must "go forth" out of Himself to be present to another, to share His being with that other. Thus God creates the whole world in order that He may share Himself through His gifts with man. Only man stands amidst all creatures as the one made "according to the image and likeness" (Gn 1:26) of God.

Only man is an *unfinished* nature that has been gifted by God with spiritual faculties to communicate with God's knowledge and love. Man can freely receive God's communications and answer God's call to become *divinized,* to be elevated into sharing by a *participation* in God's very nature (2 P 1:4). The aim for which God has created us is that we might enter into a living union in knowledge and love with Him and in Him to find our complete happiness.

DEIFICATION

Thus the early Fathers saw our fulfilled human nature as one in Jesus Christ. He is the image of the invisible God (Col 1:15) and we have been made in and through that image (Jn 1:2). "God's love for us was revealed when God sent into the world his only Son so that we could have life through him" (1 Jn 4:9). The redeeming work of the crucified and risen Jesus consists in giving us His Spirit of love through whom we may know the Father and the fullness of the Son (Jn 17:3) and thus we ourselves can become truly children of God (Jn 1:12; Rm 8:15; Ga 4:6).

This "going-forth" of God, to use Pseudo-Dionysius' term, is simply *grace* in the primal sense. It is God in His *hesed* covenantual love, pursuing His people as He stretches out His "two hands—Jesus Christ and the Holy Spirit" as St. Irenaeus in the second century was fond of saying.

All of God's creative, loving energies are focused upon the mystery of God's free choice of us to become His holy people in Christ Jesus.

> Before the world was made, he chose us,
> chose us in Christ,
> to be holy and spotless, and to live through love in his
>   presence,
> determining that we should become his
> adopted sons, through Jesus Christ
> for his own kind purposes,
> to make us praise the glory of his grace,
> his free gift to us in the Beloved,
> in whom, through his blood, we gain our
> freedom, the forgiveness of our sins (Ep 1: 4-7).

God, therefore, is grace as He goes out of Himself in His uncreated energies to share His very own life with us. We can, then, truly know God and experience Him. Although in His Godhead He is totally incomprehensible, yet in His energies, He can be experienced. The whole message of the Good News consists in God's revelation of Himself as a loving Father, giving Himself to us through His Son Jesus in His Spirit and also in the fact that such a recreating relationship of God towards us can be truly experienced by us. In that experience we can know God in His love-toward-us. And we can cooperate with God's loving energies to be loving energies toward others. If we cannot first "experience" God's love for us (which is the essence of *contemplation*), we will never be able to give true, self-sacrificing love to others. And without genuine love man dies!

THE NATURE OF GOD'S ENERGIES

God's energies, therefore, are really God in His loving relationships toward us. In God His activities can never be divided into those that are *sacred* and those that are merely *secular,* between those that are *natural* and those that are *supernatural.* The energies are God, who is His essence is unapproachable and simple, yet who in His condescending love is *always* (hence *uncreated*) manifesting Himself to us in diverse ways. They are God's showing Himself in self-giving to us human beings.

Archbishop Joseph Raya gives us a beautiful description of God's energies that summarizes well the Greek patristic teaching:

> It is not God's action but God himself in his action who makes himself known to man and gives him the ability to "see" him. God enters into man's love, remaining there in his intimate reality. This presence is real, indeed most real. This communication of God himself is called, "Uncreated Energy." The uncreated energies of God are not 'things' which exist outside of God, not 'gifts' of God; they are God himself in his action. They are the very God who is himself Uncreated. They are therefore called 'uncreated' because their cause and origin is the Essence of God. In them God as it were, goes beyond himself and becomes 'transradiant' in order to really communicate himself. Thus the Essence and energies of God are not 'parts' of

God but two ways by which we human beings can contemplate God's essence.[7]

In such a biblical and patristic vision *grace* is not
primarily a "thing" that God places upon our nature to
give us "something" extrinsic in order to perfect our being. Grace is God's presence as activating love. His love is
always present, permeating us, surrounding us, drawing us
in all things by His love into greater oneness with Him. The
energies are God in loving and creative relationships to
share His holiness and inner life with us. They are not the
created relationships that result from God's loving activities but they are truly *God-in-action* for us.

We find a description in the Book of Habakkuk of
God's energies:

> Eloah is coming from Teman,
> and the Holy One from Mount Paran.
> His majesty veils the heavens,
> the earth is filled with his glory.
> His brightness is like the day,
> rays flash from his hands,
> that is where his power lies hidden (Hab 3: 3-4).

Yahweh is an omnipresent God who by His creative Word
fills all creatures and brings them into being (Ps 33: 5-90).
Where can we ever escape from God's Spirit? (Ps 139:7).
The Prophet Jeremiah presents a God that fills all things:

> Can anyone hide in a dark corner
> without my seeing him?—it is Yahweh who speaks,
> Do I not fill
> heaven and earth?—it is Yahweh who speaks (Je 23:
> 23-24).

LOVING ENERGIES

The energies of God flow out from the three Persons within the Trinity. They are real (although not material nor merely an intellectual concept). They are essential, i.e. not an accident but they flow truly from the essence of the Godhead. Yet they are distinct from the actual essence of the Godhead.[8] These energies are essentially personified. They are the whole Trinity acting in loving relationships toward all creatures.

In such a vision we can readily see that for the Greek Fathers God can never be static in His activities toward us and His created worlds. Because the energies are personalized, they are a common manifestation of the Persons of the Trinity. If God's energies were not personalized, man would not truly share in God's very own life through His self-giving. He would not be truly regenerated into a sharer of God's very own life. Grace, then, would be a thing God heaps upon man, different from His own being. Man would be divinized only in an extrinsic way and not by direct contact with God's very own life.

Nor are we divinized in a Hindu or Buddhist fashion of non-duality (*Advaita*) where man is assimilated into the Godhead, losing any human uniqueness as a drop of water flows into the ocean.

A CONVERSION EXPERIENCE

God is, therefore, permeating all persons, all things, all events by His personalized, loving, uncreated energies. Everything is "graced" by God at each moment. It is for man, the contemplative, to have new eyes to see the loving presence of God in His Trinitarian energies in all creatures, in every event.

G. M. Hopkins beautifully captures this presence of God in nature and the need on man's part to "behold" that energizing, loving presence:

> And the azurous hung hills are his world-wielding shoulder
> Majestic-as a stallion stalwart, very-violet-sweet!
> These things, these things were here and but the beholder
> Wanting; which two when they once meet,
> The heart rears wings bold and bolder
> And hurls for him, O half hurls earth for him off under
> his feet.[9]

Such a contemplative "sees" God progressively more and more in all creatures and in all events. But it is only through a purification process that the Greek Fathers call *praxis* that one can see the energies of God bathe the whole universe and charge it with His infinite love.

It is what Teilhard de Chardin calls "passionate indifference." It is a passionate seeking of the loving Father's face in each event and a total detachment from one's own impetuous control over such an event. Such a mental balance, an interiorly disciplined control to bring all moods and feelings under God's dominance, is what St. Paul describes: "Every thought is our prisoner, captured to be brought into obedience to Christ" (2 Co 10:5).

It is a constant living in faith that strips the covering away from the experience of the moment to reveal God's loving, dynamic, energetic presence at the heart of matter. Through such faith and a child-like trust in God, such a Christian surrenders to God's love, present in every place, in each event at each moment.

A CONTINUAL GROWTH

We begin to see the importance of the asceticism of our daily lives, so full of banality at time, of monotony, boredom, at times even seemingly a dull meaninglessness. There are also moments that seem positively self-fulfilling in our daily work, our human relationships, our moments of recreation. But it is in such a daily context that we are to discover God pouring Himself out to us by His divine energies—always that He might share with us His own life and happiness.

It is easy to see, therefore, that the very nature of grace as God's life within us presupposes growth. When have we received enough of God's own life? When have we exhausted finding God working actively out of love for us in each new event? Each moment brings the exciting possibility of new growth, dependent upon our surrender to God's loving activity in each event. To accept God's loving presence *now* means to become more open to His loving presence in the next moment.

St. Gregory of Nyssa writes: "The grace of the Holy Spirit is given to everyone with the understanding that there is to be an augmenting and increase of what is received."[10]

BODILY INTEGRATION

If God, then, is present in all things with His loving activity, it should follow that, as we enter into such a spiritual, *faithful* contemplation of His energizing presence everywhere, we should see God working in our very own bodies to bring them into a harmony as St. Paul speaks of, of "spirit, soul and body" (1 Th 5:23). The biblical presentation of man is to contrast the man of the flesh (*sarx*), i.e., one living only for himself, not *in* Christ, and the Christian graced by the Holy Spirit. "Material" and "immaterial" in a Platonic dichotomy of opposites is not found in Holy Scripture.

As man opens totally to God on all levels of spirit, soul and body relationships, God's "graceful" energies elevate man into an integration as a child of God. Jesus was the most integrated human being because He found His Heavenly Father working in loving activity in all such relationships. He did not discover the Father solely loving Him in His spirit, but He was also working in and through the body of Jesus. And Jesus could enjoy the Father's love in *being* there, in His body. His body was also the *place* where the Father's energies were at work.

Jesus, therefore, used His body as a gift to communicate God's Spirit in love to all whom He met. If St. Paul could write to his fellow Christians: "Your body, you know, is the temple of the Holy Spirit" (1 Co 6:19), how much more must have Jesus known the sacredness of His body? The whole man Jesus was the Son of God.

Thus we also are to be whole persons, growing ever into a greater likeness to Christ by grace, by God's uncreating energies. Such a holistic approach, as taught by the Greek Fathers, is summarized by St. Gregory Palamas (+1359):

> The spiritual joy that comes from the spirit into the body is not at all broken by communion with the body, but transforms the body and makes it spiritual, for then it rejects all the evil appetites of the flesh, and does not drag the body down any more but rises up with it so that the

whole man becomes "Spirit" according to what is written: "He who is born of the Spirit is Spirit" (Jn 3: 6, 8).[11]

An important conclusion to the truth that, if God's energies touch also man in his bodily relationships, then the body also can experience the effects of God's loving activities. Our Platonic or Jansenistic concept of the body as something basically evil, or at least not very sacred, must change to a more incarnational view. Such a view should change our attitudes toward our bodiliness and encourage us in the way we feed and clothe our bodies, in the way we find God in our sexuality, even in the way we can use the body to pray to God.

DIAPHANOUS MATTER

The repercussions of a spirituality that "sees" God working in the material world through His loving energies are great for our daily living. If God is so present and always acting in the material world by His energies, can we, then, speak of a distinction between the sacred world and that of the profane? Can any creature in itself be objectively "profane?" Does not the term secular apply to a person who fails to see God inside" of matter? Is not the whole world sacred for the contemplative who sees God shining through that world in a diaphany?

For such contemplatives in touch with the reality of God, present everywhere in His loving energies, the world is never merely natural, waiting for God to put upon material creatures His "supernatural" grace. "The world is charged with the grandeur of God. It will flame out, like shining from shook foil."[12]

Gerard Manley Hopkins once wrote a fitting description of God's uncreated energies. "All things are charged with love, are charged with God and if we know how to touch them, give off sparks and take fire, yield drops and flow, ring and tell of him."

God's creative presence shines like a light to such contemplatives. They see how each creature tumbles forth continually through God's own personal, loving involvement. They do not seek to exploit or conquer nature, but rather, in an attitude of ever-increasing receptivity, they seek to discover God in all things and all things in God. They wish to serve Him and to render Him more adored and glorified throughout the entire universe.

A GIFT FROM GOD

To see God in all His omnipresent, creative presence and to love and adore Him in all His works is a gift of contemplation given us by God. Teilhard de Chardin well describes this intuitive grasp of God as a seeing and a taste, but above all as a gift:

> The perception of the divine omnipresence is essentially a seeing, a taste, that is to say, a sort of intuition bearing upon certain superior qualities in things. It cannot, therefore, be attained directly by any process of reasoning, nor by any human artifice. It is a gift, like life itself, of which it is undoubtedly the supreme experimental perfection . . . To experience the attraction of God, to be sensible of the beauty, the consistency and the final unity of being, is the highest and at the same time the most complete of our 'passivities of growth.' God tends, by the logic of

His creative effort, to make Himself sought and perceived by us . . . His prevenient grace is therefore always on the alert to excite our first look and our first prayer. But in the end the initiative, the awakening, always come from Him, and whatever the further developments of our mystical faculties, no progress is achieved in this domain except as the new response to a new gift.[13]

Through such a gift of contemplation, God allows us to move through this world with a childlike spirit of wonderment. God is everywhere present! We pierce through the ordinary, the prosaic, even the brokenness and sordidness of this world to "unveil" the loving presence of God inside of matter. A worshipful reverence, a taste for the sublime comes over us in the most casual events because the Spirit of God speaks to us in "the silent allusion of things to a meaning greater than themselves," as writes Abraham J. Heschel.[14]

LOVE FOR OTHERS

God's greatest display of uncreated energies is found in His loving presence within human friendships. Here God's Spirit reaches the fullness of the creative process as He works to bring two or more gathered together in Christ's name (Mt 18:20) into a greater oneness in the Body of Christ. Paradoxically the Spirit creates also, besides the experience of multiplicity in unity, the profound sense of the uniqueness of each person loving and being loved.

"God is love and anyone who lives in love lives in God and God lives in him" (I Jn 4:16). The more deeply we move in loving relationships towards others, the more deeply we experience God's activating love within us. The peak of true contemplation of God's energies is to experience His loving energies as the moving force in our free surrender in tender, loving care for others.

As we consciously seek to yield to God's loving presence in each human encounter, we are swept up into the heart of God's very own love, being poured out in a fresh release through our free cooperation. It is truly God's very own life and love as one energy force within us, empowering us with a transforming love to release that same uncreated energy of love potentially stored up in the heart of each person we meet.

Thus we come to the great paradox of the mystery of God's love as uncreated energies. God's love is uncreated, always present, always loving. Yet these great energies of God's love for His children cannot be discovered and released except through His loving children. God, so powerful, so independent and transcendent over all His creatures, has humbly tied Himself and the manifestation of His love to us human beings.

We are truly called to be "reconcilers" of the whole world as St. Paul speaks of those who are "in Christ Jesus" (2 Co 5:18). God is uniting the multiplied world into the Body of Christ through His uncreated energies experienced in prayer as personal love that He has for the individual. God becomes energized, personalized love for His world as we become signs of the new creation by those very energies of love experienced within our lives.

As we allow those energies to shine forth from our lives into the lives of others through the love we have towards others, God becomes Love manifested in His world.

One who has experienced grace as God's personal, loving presence within himself, is impelled by God's energies of love to be oriented outwardly towards others. Heaven is no longer a *place* to go to after death. It is a process of yielding to the inner, transforming power of God's love, living within all who are in Christ Jesus. Such transfigured Christians go into the world, not only to bring the creative energies of God, but also to "unconceal" His loving energies already present in His world.

They do not wait for a Heaven to come, but, in loving responsibility to God, they release His loving energies within the human scene that, by God's providence, they are privileged in time and space to be a part of. Thomas Merton speaks of our response to God as a responsibility to our world: "It is only in assuming full responsibility for our world, for our lives and for ourselves that we can be said to live really for God.[15]

God as uncreated energies of love is always calling us to be a loving energy in our world. Heaven is already this wonderful world, as seen by faith, hope and love, as bathed in God's transfiguring power of love. But it is also a return of loving energy on our part to cooperate with God's love to bring this world into the Body of Christ. This is true contemplation. It begins in experiencing God's energies of love transforming us in prayer, alone with God, into loved children of the Heavenly Father. It continues as a movement outwardly into the material world where we contemplate God's presence in an active surrender of ourselves to be His energizing love toward all whom we meet. God's uncreated energies ultimately are manifested in loving, humble service to each other. It is only such loving service that can release the energies of God's presence in our world so that they can become the transfiguring force to fulfill with human cooperation God's eternal plan to bring all things into a oneness with Christ. " . . . because God wanted all perfection to be found in him and all things to be reconciled through him and for him" (Col 1: 19-20).

3

Eyes To See God Everywhere

Jesus came into our world as Light shining in darkness. The darkness did not comprehend this Light. It even sought to extinguish it (Jn 1:5; 9-11). This is the work of the Risen Jesus: to fulfill the prophecies of old that God would heal His people of their blindness.

> But I will make the blind walk along the road
> and lead them along paths.
> I will turn darkness into light before them
> and rocky places into level tracks.
> . . . Listen, you deaf!
> Look and see, you blind! (Is 42: 16-18)

We Christians have been called by Christ to see Him everywhere as the Light of God's loving presence. We have been chosen to be a light to those who stil sit in darkness. Jesus still walks this earth in each man, woman and child whom we meet. The creative power of God tumbles forth from the lips of the Almighty Creator as He speaks His word. That Word, spoken in the flowers, the trees, birds, animals, the beauties of each new season, the sun, moon, stars, the mountains, lakes, oceans, goes forth and shall not return empty (Is 55:11). Truly not only "by the word of the Lord the heavens were made" (Ps 33:6), but the whole created world has been created in God's Word (Col 1:16). Nothing exists or moves to perfection except by God's creative power immanently present in all things. "In him we live and move and have our being" (Ac 17:28).

Yet do we really see God everywhere? Can God not complain that we, who have been given the responsibility, not only to believe in His omnipresence but also to see Him there by faith and point out His presence to others, have failed because of our blindness to the light of His presence? "I am God . . . the Holy One present among you" (Hos 11:9). Yet God can so often accuse us

> My watchmen are blind,
> all of them unaware;
> they are all dumb dogs,
> they cannot bark,
> dreaming as they lie there
> loving their sleep (Is 56:10).

We see and yet we do not see. We see beautiful flowers and fail to see the beautiful face of God shining through the flowers. We see men and women, as the blind man of Bethsaida confessed, as "trees walking" (Mk 8:24). So much of God's loving presence walks into our lives each day, at each moment, but we fail to see Him. We are "invaded" constantly by God's energizing love in each event. Yet most of us are asleep to that presence. Jesus still shouts out to us: "Why are you sleeping? Wake up!" (Lk 22:46).

LORD, THAT I MAY SEE

The composer of Mark's Gospel must have been aware of the *kerygmatic* or preached values contained in the account of Jesus' healing of the blind Bartimaeus on the road to Jericho. This blind man, like us, sat on the roadside of life, blind to much of the real world that passed him and us. He hears that Jesus is passing by and he hopes that this miracle-worker of Nazareth will free him from his blindness.

He shouts out: "Jesus, Son of David, have pity on me!" Those around him seek to silence him but he shouts all the louder that Jesus show pity on him. We see how Jesus gives a call that the blind man come to Him and we hear the enthusiastic response of Bartimaeus. God in Jesus is also always asking us as He asks the blind man: "What do you want me to do for you?"

"Master, I want to see." Jesus simply answered such a request, filled with expectant hope and faith: "Be on your way. Your faith has healed you." The blind man opened his eyes to see God's Word before him. The story ends with the significant words: "Immediately he received his sight and started to follow Jesus up the road" (Mk 10: 46-52).

SEEING BY REASON

The first step in "seeing" God is to use our imagination, emotions, intellect and will to order the truths of the Christian faith. St. Paul teaches that all men, by the use of their reasoning powers, can come to know God as "visible."

Ever since God created the world his everlasting power and deity—however invisible—have been there for the mind to see in the things he has made. That is why such people are without excuse: they knew God and yet refused to honor him as God or to thank him; instead, they made nonsense out of logic and their empty minds were darkened (Rm 1: 20-21; cf. also: Ws 13:1).

But God has so loved the world that He personally has entered into the heart of the world and has become truly man, a part of our world. God's holiness is proved by His personal, involving love in wanting to break into our history by means of His only begotten Son.

We, as Christians, have a greater source of knowledge of God, of "seeing" God in His Word, than those who do not accept in faith the doctrine of the Holy Trinity. The Bible is God's revealing Word that has come down from the Father to teach us about Him. There is no way of knowing the Father but through His Son. It is imperative, therefore, if we wish to *see* God in His objective truth concerning His own revealed nature, man's beginning and end and the means to use to obtain man's end, that we immerse ourselves in God's revealed Word found in Holy Scripture.

Writers on prayer describe the first stages of mental prayer (transcending from vocal prayer) as *discursive* prayer or meditation. In Christian meditation the accent is on one's mental involvement in bringing the memory, imagination, will and intellect to focus in concentration upon a Christian truth or a passage from Scripture of the teachings and actions of the men and women whose lives, especially of Jesus Christ, are recorded in the Old and New Testaments.

The object of such mental prayer is to become "present" to God, through a past, historical moment. The text of Scripture becomes a sign of the presence of God and the divine action towards us. By a deepening of the Holy Spirit's gift of faith, hope and love, we move from historical considerations, the *chronos* or historical time, to the *kairos,* the eternal *now* of God. As we experience God's present, loving action toward us, our discursive activities yield to an affective response on our part to God's loving presence towards us.

Through faith we "see" God in His scriptural Word. The historical Word, His teachings and actions, become for us the normative values that allow us to move into deeper levels of "seeing" God beyond His scriptural Word by encountering the living power of the presence of the Risen Christ. The same Jesus Christ, alive today, begins to work upon us, as we move away from the historical details found in Scripture to reach the actual, living event *now* of this Person, Jesus Christ. He is meeting us *now* as we open ourselves in loving surrender to His activity.

SEEING GOD AFFECTIVELY

As our faith in God's loving activities opens us up to His presence as powerfully experienced in our period of mental prayer, we are moved by various affections that flow spontaneously from our hearts toward the Holy Trinity, found immanently within us and also in the world around us. It is especially Jesus Christ who is now seen as present to us in our daily lives in an attraction, never before so affectionately experienced.

Jesus seems so close to us as we yearn to be present to Him throughout our daily activities. Our heart spontaneously, with great ease and no apparent effort on our part, seeks His face in places of our daily lives, hitherto closed to our knowledge of His presence. Everything cries out to us that God is here present in Jesus, His incarnate Word. Affections and great yearning for Jesus flow out of us in our morning prayer and continue with ardent feeling throughout the day.

Aspirations pour from our heart that reveal the hunger within us for greater union with God. A word, a phrase from Scripture will return spontaneously to our lips and serve as a springboard to the loving presence of the Lord. Especially the name of Jesus comes forth from our heart with ease and joy. We find Jesus present in each person we meet. His love covers us, even in events that formerly were judged to be unpleasant and negative. Our values of what is important take on a more evangelical tone as we strive to simplify our desires, tastes, thoughts, deeds and words according to the mind of Christ as given in the New Testment.

OH GOD!

In a delightful recent movie called "Oh God!" the actor, George Burns, plays the part of God. He appears wearing a baseball cap and tennis shoes, smoking a cigar and looking very ordinary. Again he mysteriously appears driving a taxicab. He seeks to teach his latter-day prophet, an assistant manager of a super-market, that God loves all of us greatly and we should look for Him in each person we meet. His message is: God is so ordinary precisely because He is so great and loving. And we, therefore, must

open our eyes to find Him in all walks of life and in all individuals.

"Oh God!" becomes a prayer of wonderment, at this
stage of prayer, so full of strong, loving affections. We
wonder at God's goodness and beauty in all of His creation, especially in the gifts of friends who now show us
more of God, or rather we now, by a deeper faith "see"
more of God's beauty in them than we had ever seen
before.

We see Him inside of His creation as a dynamic,
energetic Lover, always giving Himself to us in amazingly
new ways. The formerly monotonous and banal activities
now become surcharged with an inner force, God's uncreated energies of love. We feel that inner power of God
in each event, releasing a healing force within us:

> . . . but those who hope in Yahweh renew their strength,
> they put out wings like eagles.
> They run and do not grow weary,
> walk and never tire (Is 40:31).

YOU SHALL DREAM DREAMS

It is in this period of affective prayer that one
develops mostly his ability to turn within, into the realm of
the spirit, and there "see" God in a deepening silence as
far as our discursive powers go. Yet our main activity
centers chiefly upon our activating our imagination in
times of meditation and also upon our study of our daily
dreams. Morton Kelsey has admirably developed the art of
activating our imagination in: *The Other Side of Silence.*[1]

He points out the value of developing our imagination in such a stage of affective prayer:

> Images come from the inner world where we have the most intimate contact with realities that are usually hidden from view in the outer world. They have the power to contact these realities and offer us ways of relating to them so that we gain the insight and drive and energy which they hold potentially for our use. Images also help us work with the emotions that are generated by these highly charged experiences of the spiritual world. When one is overwhelmed by a negative experience of this realm, it is almost impossible to get at the root of the problem without images that will show us what the negative force is and then enable us to bring God or the Risen Christ into the picture by the use of the imagination.[2]

St. Ignatius in his *Spiritual Exercises* encourages the retreatant to such a mode of prayer in the second week, especially when he outlines the contemplation on the nativity by the use of one's senses. The retreatant is asked to enter into the historical scene recorded in the Gospel, to be present to the *personae dramatis* in the most vivid way by picturing the cave, seeing the animals, smelling the straw, etc., hearing what the persons involved in the nativity scene are saying. By using the five senses in a creatively, imaginative way, the retreatant is brought powerfully into the presence of God and His communicating love that allows for a free flow of ardent affections, designated to direct our will to a more complete surrender of ourselves to God, to grow, in St. Ignatius' words, "in personal devotedness."

Dreams can be a powerful help also to "see" God in His communication with us. This is true for all of our life time, but especially true at this stage of growing in prayer to be more receptive to God's activity upon us, in our past life that opens up to His present and future operations within the context of our existential lives. Holy Scripture has consistently presented dreams as a very important mode of God's communication with human beings. Modern Christianity is slowly regaining this lost art of dream analysis, especially through the pioneer work of Carl G. Jung. He wrote about the value of dreams:

> The analysis of dreams is an art, a technique, a science of the psychological life; it is not a game but a practical method of inestimable value to those who learn its language.[3]

A third of our lives is spent in sleeping and in dreams. The importance of dreams to the dreamer's physical health has been incontrovertibly established. Sleep laboratories at centers like the University of Chicago, New York University, Cornell, Duke and other places discover for us the patterns of dreams and sleep. Jung and his followers have taught those who are interested how to interpret the various symbols discovered occurring in dreams and have shown how dreams are indispensable tools for self-knowledge. Dreams are means of listening to God as He advises, corrects, punishes, comforts, heals and warns us. God's communication to us is the prime purpose why we dream. It is for us to tune into this valuable way of "seeing" God.

In such communication God speaks in images, a pictorial, sensual language, that is non-verbal and pre-logical. Dr. Maria Mahoney insists that the unconscious launches a dream to "wake up" the dreamer to some aspect of his or her conscious life or personal attitudes about which he or she is sound asleep.[4]

This is especially true in the deep-level, archetypal dreams. At the stage of prayer that we are describing as affective prayer in which images are important to bring us into the presence of God's communication, a study of our daily dreams through recording them in a journal can become an important means of growing in a "listening" to God acting deeply within our interior. Dr. Ira Progoff gives through his *Journal Workshop* a practical method for using the "Intensive Journal."[5]

OUT OF THE OASIS

The intense affections produced in this stage of prayer change our prayer-life. Deeper faith and trust are poured into our hearts through the love of God experienced, not only in times of solitary prayer, but also in the midst of our nitty-gritty tasks of daily life. There is a perception, deep and peaceful, inside of us and outside, of God's loving presence. It is like soft music playing unceasingly in the background. It is like a strong, gentle voice, attracting, drawing us with deep love into a greater union.

Before there was seeing God by our discursive thinking. Now there is a knowledge of *presence*. We have entered into a new form of knowing and experiencing God. It is not knowing through concepts. It is now more a way of knowing by active receptivity. We become more gentle and docile to His energies working in us and around us.. We are no longer as aggressive as before in our dealings with others, because we begin to *see* beyond the exterior appearances, the *persona* in them, to perceive something of the *true* person in them as loved by God in their unique beauty and inner mobility.

Such a global presence of God, bringing us great joy and strong affections, especially in our concentrated period of prayer, eventually gives way to a call to a new way of seeing God. The strong, loving affections begin to merge into one single attitude of faith. This is not an assent to a revealed truth, but rather a complex of all virtues merging into a total surrender to the workings of God. Affections that once flowed freely upon considerations of God's attributes now seemingly dry up. Aridity takes over. One's intellect seems impotent to "see" God through any discursive activity.

St. John of the Cross describes the transition into the prayer of *faith*:

> The third and surest sign is that a person likes to remain alone in loving awareness of God, without particular considerations, in interior peace and quiet and repose, and without the acts and exercises (at least discursive, those in which one progresses from point to point) of the intellect, memory and will; and that he prefers to remain only in the general, loving awareness and knowledge we mentioned, without any particular knowledge or understanding.[6]

FEAR OF THE UNKNOWN

From my personal experience in dealing with the stages of prayer that lay persons, priests and religious undergo, I find very many serious, prayerful persons reaching this state, after the verdant, refreshing oasis of affective prayer, and stopping just short of the desert. They seem afraid to push into a level of prayer that calls for a deepening of faith,a letting go of one's control through discursive activity, a more complete surrender to allow God to "appear" in prayer as He wishes.

It is an advanced form of prayer, the beginning of true contemplation, where images and words tend to disappear and God is free to speak His Word in a new way. It is *seeing* God by not seeing Him through concepts. But most human beings have an instinctive fear of the unknown.

Carl Jung has pointed out repeatedly how difficult it is for human beings to become self-recollected. Man is predominantly unconscious of the deeper layers of his being. Hence he has an invincible dread of becoming more conscious of himself. It is the fear of encountering what *The Cloud of Unknowing* calls "the naked being." Only by confronting this deep-down core of one's being can man attain a unity with God.

Yet entering into this interior desert is the only way to enter into greater life, greater communication with God beyond any images or words. It necessitates a dying to our own control within prayer and a yielding through the power of the Holy Spirit to God's communication of His Word in a more direct, immediate experience in sheer faith, hope and love. Thomas Merton has well described the paradox of emptiness and filling, of death and new life:

> All the paradoxes about the contemplative way are reduced to this one: being without desire means being led by a desire so great that it is incomprehensible. It is too huge to be completely felt. It is a blind desire, which seems like a desire for "nothing" only because nothing can content it. And because it is able to rest in no-thing, then it rests, relatively speaking, in emptiness. But not in emptiness as such, emptiness for its own sake. Actually there is no such

entity as pure emptiness and the merely negative emptiness of the false contemplative is a "thing" not a "nothing." The "thing" that it is is simply the darkness of self, from which all other beings are deliberately and of set-purpose excluded.

But true emptiness is that which transcends all things, and yet is immanent in all. For what seems to be emptiness in this case is pure being. It is not this, not that. Whatever you say of it, it is other than what you say. The character of emptiness, at least for a Christian contemplative, is pure love, pure freedom. Love that is free of everything, not determined by any thing or held down by any special relationship. It is love for love's sake. It is a sharing, through the Holy Spirit, in the infinite charity of God. And so when Jesus told His disciples to love, He told them to love as universally as the Father who sends His rain alike on the just and the unjust. "Be ye perfect as Your Heavenly Father." This purity, freedom and indeterminateness of love is the very essence of Christianity. It is to this above all that monastic prayer aspires.[7]

And yet there are so few spiritual directors who will encourage and guide people, hungry for deeper prayer, to move into such a prayer of faith, the beginning of true contemplation. It should not be considered as an exceptional state of prayer, given to few persons. God is everywhere present and eagerly seeking to communicate Himself to all of us.

THE CONTEMPLATIVE LIFE

Such a "seeing" God everywhere admits of great degrees of purity of heart. Contemplation is not, therefore, an objective reality that comes upon us suddenly on a given day or after we have faithfully observed certain techniques of breathing, sitting, the use of chant, dance or a silently pronounced mantra. Contemplation is a flowering of a deeper identity of ourselves on an entirely different level of consciousness than any mere psychological discovery. It comes as a slow process of growth as a gift from the Holy Spirit who infuses into our total being the gifts of increased faith, hope and love. These virtues bring us into a new knowledge of God's presence, living and lovingly acting within us by His Trinitarian indwelling and also by His transcendent presence in all things outside of us. But such a gift of contemplating God "inside" of all things is also a gift to purify ourselves. At the heart of love is a constant, dying process, a readiness to "let go" of our self-centered world and embrace greater life in a risk of faith, trust and love. More and more our progress in true prayer becomes tied to our life-situation. Like Abraham we enter into a journey of faith. "Leave your country, your family and your father's house for the land I will show you" (Gn 12:1).

THE DESERT

We do not like to surrender to God's gentle leading. Thomas Merton quotes Gabriel Marcel on the "dread" we experience before we can let go of our own self-possession.

> Following Gabriel Marcel, dread divests itself of the sense of possession, of having our being and our power to live, in order that we may simply be in perfect openness, turned inside out, of the defenselessness that is utter simplicity, and total gift.[8]

It is at this point that one chooses like Abraham to be guided totally by faith in God and to push further into the darkening of our own intellectual control over what is happening or to cling to our own way of following God. If we choose consistently the latter course, we will resist God's loving activities in our lives. We will negate His grace. We simply will be attached to ourselves and not be docile and surrendering to God.

How often inadequate spiritual direction will add to such spiritual cowardliness to destroy the beginnings of a true call to contemplation. This can happen when a spiritual director encourages a person to stay on a prayer level that demands less naked faith, namely, to return to a discursive or image-activating meditation. Much harm has been done by spiritual directors who, lacking true contemplative experience, encourage such persons to "do" things in prayer. Such a busyness defeats any further surrender to God in utter emptiness.

THEORIA PHYSICA

Many books have been written about the "prayer of faith."[9] I would like to present briefly some insights from the Greek Fathers, especially from St. Maximus the Confessor, who present the prayer of faith in a more positive vision of discovering God inside of all things. It develops in conjunction with the degree of our purity of heart and humble readiness to listen and to see God's Logos working in all events.[10]

The Greek Fathers, great mystics, who penetrated into the inner presence of God in His uncreated energies of love working in nature, in Holy Scripture and the Church and through the indwelling of the individual human person, developed the transcendence of God, the ineffable Creator, holy and perfect in His essence as well as the centrality of man in the created world as the co-creator with God. Man possesses in his intellect and will the seeds of a likeness to God through grace. The Fathers stress that Jesus Christ is not only the perfect model, the Image of the Father according to whom man and the whole cosmos were created, but that through His Incarnation and His Resurrection He is also in the midst of the material world exerting His paschal victory to bring the whole created order into its fullness through the instrumentality of other human beings. We freely return love for His love in a synergy of action in union with the mind of God Himself.

The great insight of St. Maximus the Confessor is that the mystery of Easter is the foundation of the world.[11] In the Resurrection is recapitulated on a macrocosmic scale what was mirrored forth in the microcosm of Jesus Christ Risen. Here is a unified view which neither conceives God in opposition to creation nor confounds God with creation. God remains different from His creation. Yet all of creation is to enter into the Divine Life through the divinization of man himself as the reconciler with Christ of the universe back to the Father in fulfillment of His eternal plan in His Logos.

St. Maximus fought to maintain the orthodoxy of the Christology of the Council of Chalcedon (451). Just as in the person Jesus Christ there existed two distinct elements, the divine and human natures, united without destroying the distinct identity of the two component elements, so too, Maximus argues, the created cosmos is composed of distinct elements, yet the whole is also fashioned into a unity. It is for man, the contemplative, who has purified his heart from all self-love to see that Jesus Christ Risen is the bond providing the unity of intelligibility and of cosmic energy (*love*) that are hidden beneath the surface of the material appearances of creatures.

Sin has caused the unity in God's universe to become splintered into antipodes of the created world as versus the uncreated God, the sensible as opposed to the intelligible, the earth against Heaven, the world and Paradise, masculine and feminine. Man who stands between Heaven and earth, possessing both spirit and matter, must first find self-unity and then perform his God-given task of mediation between the rest of the created cosmos and its Creator. It is through the Logos-made-man that we human beings can effect this unity, first within our own lives, then through our Christified, divinized natures, within the cosmos.

SEEING GOD IN THE *LOGOI*

We have much to gain from a study of St. Maximus' doctrine of a Logos mysticism as the first stage of true contemplation. It does away with the whole problem of acquired and infused contemplation and also prevents any attempt on our part to see the prayer of faith solely in its negative aspects of seeing God only through the gift of faith in utter darkness. Such a theory of contemplation has little to offer a modern Christian by way of finding God within the materiality of his or her daily life in a very material world.

The mysterious and deifying presence of Christ the Logos is in the world exercising His loving power in the creation of all things, in Scripture and the Church's preaching of the Word and, finally, in the risen life given to those who live in Him. This moves us to a holistic view of contemplation that urges us to find the Logos of God in each event, in each creature, beginning with ourselves. What is meant by the Logos? St. John the Evangelist, St. Justin, St. Irenaeus, Clement of Alexandria, Origen, St. Athanasius and St. Gregory of Nyssa had used the Logos doctrine to explain the incarnational activity of Jesus Christ in the cosmos. St. John, working out of the Old Testament *sophianic* literature, writes:

> In the beginning was the Word:
> the Word was with God
> and the Word was God.
> He was with God in the beginning.
> Through him all things came to be,
> not one thing had its being but through him.
> All that came to be had life in him
> and that life was the light of men,
> a light that shines in the dark,
> a light that darkness could not overpower (Jn 1: 1-5).

St. Paul also had captured the centrality of the pre-existent Logos as the exemplar and efficient cause of all creation:

> . . . for in him were created
> all things in heaven and on earth:
> everything visible and everything invisible,
> Thrones, Dominations, Sovereignties, Powers—
> all things were created through him and for him.
> Before anything was created, he existed,
> and he holds all things in unity.
> Now the Church is his body,
> he is its head (Col 1: 16-18).

If all things were created in the Logos, then there is a *logos* in each creature, in you and in me, in a tree, in that beautiful, special sunset of yesterday that has its fullness in the Logos. Lars Thunberg describes the concept that St. Maximus had of the *logoi*:

> The *logos* denotes the created existence of a thing as founded in God's will that it should be; it is the principle of its coming to be and implies a participation in God as being.[12]

The *logos* of each creature is its principle of harmony that shows us the relationship of a given creature to God's total order of salvation. The whole world is interlocked and interrelated, but rational man alone is capable of seeing the harmonious relationship between the *logoi* and the Logos. It is man alone who can contemplate the presence of the Logos working within all of creation to bring with man's cooperation each creature into "spirit," namely, into the fulfillment of that particular creature's *logos* within the Divine Mind from all eternity. There is a movement, therefore, towards fulfillment. Man's free will is exercised through a prayerful contemplative spirit to receive the Spirit of the Risen Jesus and to perceive reality as existing according to the eternal Mind of God.[13]

The Logos is Jesus Christ, as an "all-powerful center, pre-containing the sources of its rays and gathering them all together."[14] All things are created through Him and all things are to be eventually reunited in Him: the Alpha and the Omega. The harmony and unity between the *logoi* and Logos is effected by us human beings who by contemplation learn to see the intelligibility "within" the created order and in love we seek to live according to God's purpose. But to *see* the *logoi* in all creatures, in all events, we must submit to the illuminating activity of the Logos. St. Maximus writes:

> Just as the sun when it rises and lights up the world manifests both itself and the things lit up by it, so the Sun of Justice, rising upon a pure mind, manifests itself and the essence of all the things that have been and will be brought to pass by it.[15]

Only such a contemplative who receives from the Logos this gratuitous gift that necessitates a slow but consistent death to self-love and attachment to worldly possesions, can see beyond the appearances and unlock the world and see the harmony existing among all creatures. He is able to enter somewhat into God's very purpose, into God's very mind, to see the *raison d'être* of each created being and then act lovingly according to that "reason."

A LOVING RESPONSE

God never gives His gifts of contemplation to us for idle pondering of God's beautiful, inner harmony. They are given as a call for us to respond to spiritualize and thus restore the entire cosmos back to God the Father through His Son in His Holy Spirit. This gift of *theoria physica,* contemplating the inner harmony of all things in God's Logos, is freely given as we surrender passively to God's presence and illumination through our very active, ascetical life of purifying our inner vision from all self-love (called *praxis* in Greek). Nevertheless, it is meant to be given to develop in us the highest kind of activity, both in loving contemplation of God and in the active apostolate to build up the Body of Christ.

Such an approach to contemplation is essentially *sophianic*. Through this gift of contemplation we are able to unite the hidden wisdom (*sophia* in Greek) of God in things with the hidden light of wisdom that we find shining within ourselves through the indwelling Trinity. The meeting and marriage of these two bring about a resplendent clarity within us and this clarity is the presence of Divine Wisdom fully recognized and active in us. Thus we should become more and more a mirror of the divine glory, the light of Christ, both shining within us and without us. This glory is resplendent with divine truth that not only exists in our mind but is lived out in our life. Such a modern prophet becomes filled with the light of wisdom which shines forth in him. God is constantly being glorified in him. At the same time he exercises a spiritualizing influence in the world by the work of his mind, his hands, his active apostolate in whatever he does, which is in accord with the creative wisdom of God in things and in history.

There cannot any longer be a purely negative attitude towards the world and what is happening in contemporary history in which we find ourselves immersed as a swimmer in a strong current of the ocean. The world is seen positively as permeated with God's uncreated energies of love. The material world is seen no longer as an obstacle that is preventing us from becoming persons of prayer. Matter is truly spiritual, both St. Maximus and Teilhard de Chardin would agree. Grace as God's loving relationships permeating all things through God's Logos and His creative Spirit of love touch us and bring us into a divinization, a union with Jesus Christ. We live in His likeness, putting on His mind in all things.

God's will is no longer a static force plunging through our lives like a cosmic steamroller and demanding a blind resignation. On the contrary, illumined by the Spirit of Jesus, we are able, progressively in the context of our daily lives, to understand the hidden purposes of the creative wisdom and the divine mercy of God in each moment and we can freely cooperate with Him as loving sons and daughters of a loving Father. God hands over to us, when we are purified and enlightened and united totally with His divine will, a progressively creative initiative of our own. This activity touches every aspect of our historical lives, the spiritual life, liturgical celebration, political and social life, art, our daily activities.

We enter into the fulfillment of the mission that God gave man in the Garden of Eden:

> Be fruitful, multiply, fill the earth and conquer it. Be masters of the fish of the sea, the birds of heaven and all living animals on the earth (Gn 1:28).

THE CHURCH

As we grow in contemplating the Logos in all creatures, we find His presence, not only within ourselves, but more and more consciously in the community of human persons, being fashioned into the one begotten Son, beloved from all eternity by His Heavenly Father. When several contemplate the Logos working within themselves and wish to surrender (the full meaning of the Christian Baptism) completely to live only according to God's Word, His Logos, the Church, the Body of Christ is being fashioned by His Holy Spirit. In this Body the living

Logos is preached and through the sacraments Jesus Christ is encountered in His resurrectional life by the Christian faithful. The end of God's indwelling within men is to effect a unity among disjointed creatures, separated from their Creator and from one another by ignorance and sin.

It is the work of the Church to achieve this unity and it does this first by unity of faith in the teachings of revelation. God has freely broken into human history. In a way God is striving, to use a bold expression that would have been understood properly by St. Maximus the Confessor and other Greek Fathers, to assume humanity in order that He might become properly Himself. As we need divinity to reach our full humanity, so God, in His free consent to give Himself to us as our loving Father, needs to become human in order to be revealed to us as God. The objectivity of God's nature and His historical relationships to mankind is not something we can subjectively dream up. God is such in His nature. He has done certain things in His historical relationships to us. Still He is constantly revealing His potential for loving us in new and exciting ways that call for our response. Subjectivism and self-delusion are overcome by obedient submission to the teaching hierarchy that Christ established over His Church.

Thus St. Maximus writes in continuity with the apostolic traditions that posit the gift of God within His Church of a teaching hierarchy:

> I cannot grieve God by keeping silent what He ordered to be spoken and confessed. For if, according to the divine Apostle, it is He Himself who has set in the Church, first apostles, secondly prophets, thirdly doctors, it is clear that he has spoken through them. By all of Holy Scripture, by

the Old and the New Testament, by the holy doctors and synods we are taught.[16]

The Church has the infallible right to preach to us the Word of God and give us the mind of Jesus Christ as this Word is to be applied to our daily lives. This Church exposes to us the Incarnate Christ, living in His glorious, resurrected life to be encountered by us through the sacraments. Baptism, administered by the Church, opens to us the fruits of the Incarnation. But it is especially in the reception of the Divine Logos and the High Priest, Jesus Christ, in the Holy Eucharist that we are deified by the fruits of His Spirit. We become able to fulfill our priestly function in His priesthood of making all things holy. As we conform ourselves to the Logos present by grace within us, we are able through the enlightenment that He gives us through His Spirit to perceive the *logoi* in other creatures and to perform the sacred role of priests (1 P 2:9) by offering a sacrifice of praise and glory to God through our proper use of creatures. Jesus Christ sacrifices Himself totally in the Eucharist to give Himself to us in order that we, through the use of our illumined reason, may be raised to the perfection of Christ.

Man stands at the center of the cosmos. Deified man, in whom God lives and through whom He acts to fulfill the world, is the mediator between the disparate and disjointed world and the unity that has been achieved perfectly in the God-Man's humanity through the Incarnation. There can be no transfiguration of the material cosmos except through human beings who themselves by grace have become divinized. Man, permeated by grace, God's loving, uncreated energies, achieves a unity within himself which allows him to effect a cosmic unity in the material world around him. Let us turn in the following chapters to develop more fully how man, the contemplative, is also man, the *doer*. Let us see how God becomes human and man becomes divine as the two meet in the Logos, Jesus Christ, as present in the materiality of our world.

4

God And Man At Work

There has been recently a renewed interest in the North American Indian and his culture. Beyond a certain collective guilt and an inner need for the white man to make reparation for the "sins" of his ancestors toward the Indians, there is something very healthy and deeply spiritual about this new interest. When we read *Black Elk Speaks,*[1] we are brought into a world reminiscent of the account of man in the Garden of Eden. It is a holistic world view, depicted by a circle, or "the sacred hoop" as Black Elk calls it.

> You have noticed that everything an Indian does is in a circle and that is because the power of the world always works in circles and everything tries to be round. In the old days when we were a strong and happy people, all our power came to us from the sacred hoop of the nation and so long as the hoop was unbroken the people flourished . . . Everything the Power of the Word does is in a circle. The sky is round and I have heard that the earth is round like a ball, and so are all the stars. The wind, in its greatest power, whirls. Birds make their nests and circles, for theirs is the same religion as ours. The sun comes up

and goes down again in a circle. The moon does the same, and both are round. Even the seasons form a great circle in their changing and always come back again to where they were. The life of man is a circle from childhood to childhood, and so is everything else where the Power moves . . . [2]

Black Elk asks: "Is not the sky a father and the earth a mother, and are not all living things with feet or wings or roots their children?"[3]

As God created the world, He meant all parts to be co-ordinated into a whole, into a dancing harmony. Man alone, created according to God's own image and likeness (Gn 1:26), was given stewardship over this wonderfully rich world. Thus God commanded man:

> Be fruitful, multiply, fill the earth and conquer it. Be masters of the fish of the sea, the birds of heaven and all living animals on the earth . . . God saw all he had made, and indeed it was very good (Gn 1: 28-31).

The world, from God's view point, therefore, is a *one*. All creatures, through the creative inventiveness and synergism of man working with God, were meant to be inter-related in a harmonious wholeness. Each part has its proper place within the whole universe. Each creature depends on and gives support to all the others in one great body, all of which has been created in and through God's Word. How beautifully this is brought out in Psalm 104:

> Yahweh, what variety you have created,
> arranging everything so wisely!
> Earth is completely full of things you have made:
> among them the vast expanse of ocean,

> teeming with countless creatures,
> creatures large and small . . .
> You give breath, fresh life begins,
> you keep renewing the world (Ps 104: 24-25, 30).

This wonderful, creating God is not only the powerful, transcendent Creator who stands above and outside of all of His creation, but He is the immanent force that lives inside of every creature. "In him we live and move and have our being" (Ac 17:28). He fills the heavens and the underworld. It is impossible to escape from His creative, sustaining Spirit (Ps 139:7).

But our Western civilization, through the deductive methods of science, has produced an anthropocentric view of the universe, of God and, therefore, of man's creativeness in his work. Once man grasped the universal laws and essences in nature, he was able to predict the way things should happen. He could invent tools to help him in the conquest of nature. The Greeks were the first to grasp the idea of knowing nature and of the relationships of man to nature. The abstract concepts of Greek philosophy and mathematical physics pushed science beyond solely a science of description of observed empirical facts. What resulted was a new way of inventing tools to allow man to control and fashion nature according to his wishes. Now man was able to determine his own values and to attain them through his inventiveness.

No longer does time, for man, possess the cyclical element. It is now a mathematical projection in a linear pattern based on the movement of the earth around the sun. A new idea of the beautiful develops, one that does not necessarily have anything to do with the real world, but with the ideal order. Beauty, as an abstract idea, is taken out of its natural environment and looked at as in Greek sculpture. It becomes a bold, detached, lifeless thing, however, enjoying perfect mathematical proportions. This is seen in Western music and painting. The mathematical perspective is found in the classical style of music of Bach, Mozart and Beethoven as well as in the photogenic painting of Raphael, Fra Angelico and Murillo. The music of Debussy seems to be a reaction to Western counterpoint music and a return to the Eastern infinite formlessness.

In such a technological, man-centered universe, nature is no longer sensed, deeply experienced in all of its individuality or imagined, but it is somehow seized through abstraction and selected for its functional usefulness. In contrast to this there is, especially among primitive peoples and romantic transcendentalists like Henry Thoreau and John Muir, the cosmo-centered universe. For the cosmo-centered man, there is a cosmic unity among all creatures. When he kills an animal or cuts a tree or plant, he seeks to restore the balance by prayer or sacrifice. Thus we find Black Elk speaking of his uprooting this cosmic oneness that he enjoyed with birds and animals:

> There was a bush and a little bird sitting in it; but just as I was going to shoot, I felt queer again, and remembered that I was to be like a relative with the birds. So I did not shoot. Then I went on down toward a creek, feeling foolish because I had let the little bird go, and when I saw a green frog sitting there, I just shot him right away. But when I picked him up by the legs, I thought: "Now I have killed him," and it made me want to cry.[3]

A THEOCENTRIC WORLD

Such a primitive, simplistic view refuses to believe that God is also in our urban societies and technological discoveries. It has not much to show modern man how, by his ingenuity and hard work, he is called to respond to God's invitation to help Him make this world into the fullness destined for it by God. Yet our anthropocentric vision is not adequate in itself as we see from the many problems caused by being too centered upon man's ideas of what is good for the entire world. Water and air pollution; the pillage of mineral resources; the increasing list of extinct or endangered species of birds and animals; the far-reaching effect of pesticides; the wanton dumping of industrial chemicals on land and sea; the overwhelming accumulation of waste, garbage and junk and, especially, the spiraling of the population explosion, all add up to instant awareness of apocalyptic crisis.[4]

Such gigantic problems are not solved primarily by more technology or more education, but by a better knowledge of man's relationships to earth, to other human beings, to himself and to God. It is a question of man's becoming rooted in God, in a *theocentric* vision of the universe, and creating a new set of values and a new system of ethics whereby man can guide his daily choices of work and pleasure by principles beyond his own self-interest. What is needed is a new theological anthropology of man as a cosmic man, a citizen—not merely of America or of earth—but of the universe.

The communications media have opened up man to the possibility of being present to a fellow-brother in drought-stricken Africa. We have literally seen men walking on the moon and suddenly planetary distances do not exist as they did before. In a moment we can be present, in a psychic way, to the needs of everyone throughout the world.

Such a planetary consciousness will make nations and individuals realize their collective responsibility for discovering and sharing knowledge about natural systems and how they are affected by man's activities and vice versa. Much work is being done in cooperative monitoring, research and study. But the greatest need and greatest urgency for a change of values is that man change his interior vision. Saving mankind from isolation and alienation will not be done by mere negative motivation through fear of a final, cataclysmic war if man does not dispel the pollution of his inner spirit. This can come only in a newness of religious insight that all men are interdependent, through a sense of community, of belonging, and sharing together the riches that God has so abundantly given to mankind. It is through interior prayer that man will be able to touch God as the Center of the "sacred hoop" and find that he meets his fellow human beings also there at the Center through his creative work done for love of God and mankind to bring about a better universe.

We need a new theological approach to man that builds our value system not on our own individual rights so much as on our personal growth through personalistic relationships with all human beings. Such a vision of the unity and inter-dependence of all of nature can never be deduced from Euclidean axioms. This is where the American Indian and the Hindu and Buddhist monks can teach us how to recapture the art of turning within and listening in order to go beyond the mere periphery of what we consider to be reality.

Carl Jung has said that Western man, if he is to save

himself from further decadence, must eventually develop his own Western form of yoga. By this he did not mean merely doing the *asanas,* Indian breathing exercises or sitting in the lotus position. He meant entering deeply within ourselves and there hearing the true Self, the Absolute Ground of all being, tell us through experiential knowledge and enlightenment, that the world of senses is not the totality of reality, but that through an experience of our own unique oneness with the indwelling God we are really one with all being.

THE WORLDLINESS OF THE WORLD

God's oneness with us and the entire world is not a naive pantheism. It is not a simplistic form of *monophysitism* which destroys the true "secularity" of the world and all its material forms of creation as the world becomes "sacralized" into a part of God. The early Christian thinkers did not despise the world but recognized it for what it truly was. It is not God. It possesses by its nature nothing of God's inner life, yet God is immanently present inside of all nature through His uncreated energies of love. The created world is not "holy"; it is not sacral. Thus a severe, yet in itself, truthful objectivity, was established in their thinking and attitudes toward the material things of this world.

But more importantly, such early Christians were able to see by their deep, contemplative spirit reflecting on Holy Scripture, especially the central mystery of their faith, namely, the Incarnation, that God sent into a "secular," not-godly world, His only Son to communicate, through His material body and, through that, through the rest of the material creation, with us. In the historical person of

Jesus Christ, God and human beings communicate in a relationship hitherto unknown. It is precisely in Christ's humanity, which is not the infinite, sacred God, the fullness of being, but it is *worldly,* distinct from God, finite, dependent totally upon God for its existence, that God can reveal His great goodness and love. Through Jesus Christ, He communicates His being to something other than Himself. In a way we can say that God needs matter and a created world in order to become fully God by communicating His great love to mankind and thus He becomes able to share in true love His life with us by making us into His divine adopted children.

A GROANING WORLD IN BONDAGE

It is revelation through Holy Scripture that teaches us what happened to God's creation that He saw was very good. That created world, as destined by God, was meant to be a reflection of the "invisible things" (Rm 1:20). Man was supposed to "inscape" into each creature and intuit the loving presence of God. Man, sharing in God's imageness, was to cooperate with God to continue the creative forces within God's creation.

But this creation, when man turned away from "inscaping" and turned toward himself as the end of his strivings, fell into a universal slavery to an extrinsic force. It was plunged into darkness, chaos and death. Man and woman would suffer in their mutual relationships and in rearing their children (Gn 3:16). Human beings would find great resistance in their efforts to develop the soil and bring the world into a perfection. Work would be no longer a joyful, creative process with God as a prayerful worship and adoration, but now man would find himself alienated from the created world around him. Sin separated man from nature around him and pitted him as an enemy that had to fight against the surrounding world as though against a terrifying enemy. The account in *Genesis* of man's attitude towards work is told in mythopoetic terms:

> Accursed by the soil because of you.
> With suffering shall you get your food from it
> every day of your life.
> It shall yield you brambles and thistles,
> and you shall eat wild plants.
> With sweat on your brow
> shall you eat your bread,
> until you return to the soil,
> as you were taken from it (Gn 3: 17-19).

St. Paul, using the apocalyptic symbols known to his Jewish traditions and also to the Gnostic sects of his day, shows the cosmic spiritual forces, external to God's intrinsically good creation, holding the universe in bondage. The Prince of the World (Jn 12:31), Satan or Belial, led the attack along with his intermediate powers, the Principalities, Powers, Thrones, Dominions. The Evil One, the god of this world (2 Co 4:4), has prevented men from seeing the splendor of Christ, who is God's image (2 Co 4:5). St. Paul writes: "And you were dead, through the crimes and the sins in which you used to live when you were following the way of this world, obeying the ruler who governs the air, the spirit who is at work in the rebellious" (Ep 2:1).

Through one man sin entered into the world (Rm 5:12) and through sin, death has spread throughout all of God's creation. This sin, basically one of pride and selfish love, subjugates man from without by using man's own physical flesh as the instrument for his estrangement from

God. Sin has produced death in all of man's works (Rm 7:15). Sin rules as king in the realm of death (Rm 5:21). This sinfulness has spread throughout all of creation. The sub-human cosmos shares the fate of man. As that world would reach its fullness through man's prayerful work, so now that world helplessly is tied to man's sinful state. Man and the cosmos were meant to be a unity. They, therefore, will have to be redeemed and fulfilled together. No part of the universe will be unredeemed when the Redeemer comes, for He is capable of uniting the universe with the Creator. St. Paul depicts this universal, cosmic bondage through man's sinfulness:

> The whole creation is eagerly waiting for God to reveal his sons. It was not for any fault on the part of creation that it was made unable to attain its purpose, it was made so by God; but creation still retains the hope of being freed, like us, from its slavery to decadence, to enjoy the same freedom and glory as the children of God. From the beginning till now the entire creation, as we know, has been groaning in one great act of giving birth; and not only creation, but all of us who possess the first-fruits of the Spirit, we too groan inwardly as we wait for our bodies to be set free (Rm 8: 19-23).

THE SECOND ADAM

But where sin did abound, there did grace more abound. What man could not accomplish in his darkness, God in His mercy set about to correct (Rm 15: 8-9; 11:32; 5:8). "God dealt with sin by sending his own Son in a body as physical as any sinful body, and in that body God condemned sin" (Rm 8:3). Christ condemned sin in the flesh through His death and resurrection whereby He passed gloriously from the state of flesh (*sarx*) to that of spirit (*pneuma*). As long as Jesus was confined to space and time through His physical bodiliness, He could not share His divine life with other men. Because He had not yet died, He could not give His Spirit of love, says St. John (Jn 7:39). But once the word of God has been definitively spoken as the Suffering Servant of Yahweh on the cross, He is able to pour out into our hearts the Spirit of love (Rm 5:5). As through His human body Christ, as an integral part of humanity touched all men, so by the resurrection of His human body the bodies of all men and the whole universe would be given the possibility to be re-oriented to God. This re-orientation would lead eventually to a full resurrection in the Spirit of every man who would open himself to the Spirit of Jesus Risen and, through man's touching of the cosmos in and through the Spirit of Jesus, the whole cosmos would be led into spirit.

Jesus Christ is now the New Adam, the perfect man, not only complete as God's image according to whom all human beings have been created, and therefore the promise of what awaits us also (Rm 5:2), but, above all, as the Head of the new humanity and of the New Jerusalem. Now Jesus is the New Adam and the Lord of the universe, capable of bestowing upon all of us the same life of the Spirit by making us children of His Heavenly Father (Rm 8:15; Ga 4:6). " . . . and he will transfigure these wretched bodies of ours into copies of his glorious body. He will do that by the same power with which he can subdue the whole universe" (Ph 3:21).

CHRIST—THE RECONCILER OF THE WORLD

In order that we may be able to find God in our work, we need to develop the faith vision that St. Paul so powerfully depicts in his last two epistles written in captivity in a Roman prison, to the Ephesians and to the Colossians. In a cosmic setting, similar to the cosmology in which St. Paul in his earlier writings depicted a universal bondage holding mankind and all of the sub-human cosmos in death and sin, he shows the full extent of Christ's dominion over all creation, visible and invisible. All creatures were created by Him and are under His dominion. They have been created for Him and are being brought into completion through His activity. Christ is now reconciling the whole world back to the Father through the Church of which He is the Head.

> He is the image of the unseen God
> and the first-born of all creation,
> for in him were created
> all things in heaven and on earth:
> everything visible and everything invisible,
> Thrones, Dominations, Sovereignties, Powers
> all things were created through him and for him.
> Before anything was created, he existed,
> and he holds all things in unity.
> Now the Church is his body,
> he is its head.
> As he is the Beginning,
> he was first to be born from the dead,
> so that he should be first in every way;
> because God wanted all perfection
> to be found in him
> and all things to be reconciled through him and for him,
> everything in heaven and everything on earth,
> when he made peace by his death on the cross (Col 1: 15-20).

Jesus Christ is the *Kyrios,* the Lord and Master of the whole universe, and all things belong to Him. "He has put all things under his feet and made him, as the ruler of everything, the head of the Church; which is his body, the fullness of him who fills the whole creation" (Ep 1: 22-23). Through the Spirit of the Risen Jesus, we have been baptized into His Body, the Church, and we are now new creatures. A whole new world, like a leaven, has been inserted into the universe. This new creation is Christ, the Head. We are the members of His Body, the saved humanity, that together must reconcile the entire world and bring it into the fullness according to the eternal plan of the Heavenly Father. Again, St. Paul depicts this newness in Christ and the obligation and power given to us to be with Him reconcilers of the entire world:

> For anyone who is in Christ, there is a new creation; the old creation has gone, and now the new one is here. It is all God's work. It was God who reconciled us to himself through Christ and gave us the work of handing on this reconciliation. In other words, God in Christ was reconciling the world to himself, not holding men's faults against them, and he has entrusted to us the news that they are reconciled. So we are ambassadors for Christ; it is as though God were appealing through us, and the appeal that we make in Christ's name is: be reconciled to God (2 Co 5: 17-20).

The Body of Christ, the redeemed humanity and the transfigured world brought about by man's cooperation with Jesus Christ, is in process of growing into its fullness (*pleroma*). This is brought out in Vatican II's *Constitution on the Church in the Modern World:* "The Church, or, in other words, the kingdom of Christ now present in mystery, grows visibly through the power of God in the world."[5] The mystical Christ has not yet attained to His full growth. He is to reach His fullness through all created activity that is under the direction of the Spirit of Jesus.

Our human dignity consists in reaching our fulfillment in working to bring about a world in progress that we thoroughly love along with the love we have for Jesus Christ, coming to full stature in His Body, the Church. The more transcendent and ultimate in concern be every thought, word and deed, the greater is our human growth, because this will be the measure of not only our love for God and neighbor but also the measure of God's very own uncreated energies of love working in us and through us to fulfill His eternal plan. But this is not a Platonic, static plan, a universal idea in the mind of God that disregards man's intervention in free cooperation with God. Man is to touch the immanence of God within all of matter and through his cooperative, synergistic labors with God's creative presence, God and man are to create this world.

GOD PRESENT WITHIN MATTER

Through a Platonism that has run through Western Christianity, we have dichotomized God from His material creation. We have placed God spatially, at least in our thinking and praying, *up there* and have forgotten the essential mystery of the Incarnation, that God pursues us, His children, by being Himself "inside" of matter. We have already pointed out God's independent existence in all of His perfect essence. Yet He is always becoming present to His creatures by His "uncreated energies of love." Before we can truly build a spirituality of work as a prayerful oneness, working together with God, we need to develop a spirituality of *presences* that will allow us to *see* God truly at the heart of matter, or better, that will allow us to *see* Him in the material world and activities that make up our daily existence.

If our Christian faith tells us that the divine presence of God, like the rays of the sun, glows within the cosmos and that through our sensate life we make contact with this material world, why, then, do we have to continue to flee the material world in order to meet the Lord? Why can we not be in a constant attitude of worship, adoration and self-surrender to God in the midst of our daily work and our constant contact with the material world that surrounds us? Our first step to find God within the context of our daily work is to become aware of the Divine Immanence in all things. This Immanence is within us and experienced in prayer. It is the same immanence within all of the material world drawing all things into a unity in God.

The second step in a spirituality of Christian worldliness in the best incarnational sense is not merely to contemplate God immanently present in all things, but for us to surrender to God who actively holds all things together (Ac 17:28). But this step leads us even more interiorly to God's presence as energetic love. God is continuously, not merely present in all things, holding them in their being, but He is constantly creating the world. God is dynamically in motion as He creates the world through human beings. It is for us to recognize by deep faith that God is actively creating in all circumstances, be they our active works or simply events that happen to us as we passively accept them. "We know that by turning everything to their good, God cooperates with all those who love him, with all those that he has called according to his purpose" (Rm 8:28).

The fourth step is to recognize by faith that God is a transforming, deifying, loving energy that is moving us and through us the entire material world into a oneness. The Kingdom of God is being fashioned by God and man working to recapitulate all of creation. This is a process that the Greek Fathers called *theosis* or divinization. God is no longer merely the *One On High* or the *Within* of things, but He is also the *Beyond*. Man sees himself at this stage of spiritual maturity as called by God to transform the earth in all of its particularity of each thing and each atom. It is only at this stage of *insight* that the Christian sees a unity between the love of God and the particularity of each atom of the universe. Matter is now sacred, as Teilhard de Chardin would preach so effectively in his many writings. He states:

> Each one of our works, by its more or less remote or direct repercussion upon the spiritual world, contributes to perfect Christ in His mystical totality.[6]

In such a faith vision, the Christian no longer moves between separated worlds, the sacred and the secular, but there is now only the vision of the Body of Christ, still being formed from the material of this world through man's creative power. This is the fifth level of Christian consciousness that leads the Christian to unite without inner strain and inner division "the passion of the earth and the passion of God."[7] This summit guides and gives meaning to each other step along the way to a true mysticism of work and prayer. It is a sheer gift of God, given to those who seek to possess it and strive each day to push themselves into greater faith, purity of heart and fidelity to God's presences as we have outlined. I have tried to present this intuitive synthesis of the whole in a work that I entitled: *The Cosmic Christ from Paul to Teilhard*.[8] It is a consciousness in one and the same act, of God and each creature in the world and their relationship. It is a penetrating act of *seeing* inside of the material world as it presents itself to our senses which allows us to go beyond the strict dualism that separates God and the world, work and prayer, and yet it does maintain the distinction that God is *not* the material world nor the material world or even we human beings are ever turned into God. The world truly becomes a *diaphany,* as Teilhard de Chardin so often describes it, of God's inner, active presence, to form the Body of Christ.

A MYSTICISM OF PRAYER AND ACTION

To make our daily work truly meaningful and fulfilling we must move in the tension, without any separation, between a forward movement, *l'En-Avant* to use Teilhard's term, of human development and progress that shows an enthusiastic hope that all actions posited in love can contribute to fulfilling also the universe, and an upward movement towards God (*l'En-Haut*). Each person, as St. Paul so eloquently speaks of the individual members of the Body of Christ, the Church, enjoys a uniqueness and talents that no one else possesses in quite the same way.

> There is a variety of gifts but always the same Spirit; there are all sorts of service to be done, but always to the same Lord; working in all sorts of different ways in different people, it is the same God who is working in all of them. The particular way in which the Spirit is given to each person is for a good purpose (1 Co 12: 4-7).

As different members of the human body have varied functions, so too, Christians have different and yet complementary vocations, pledging themselves in a variety of degrees of intensity to action, prayer or both together (Cf.: 1 Co 12: 12-30). The material world has been called by God to achieve its fulfillment in the cosmic Christ, the fulfilled Risen Jesus Christ as Head and saved humanity as His members. Through both the Head and the members the whole material world is to attain a place within the spiritualized Body of Christ. The entire universe is to be recapitulated by the Whole Christ back to the Heavenly Father.

All human persons are called, therefore, to build the earth into the Heavenly Jerusalem, the fully realized Body of Christ. By faith poured into our hearts by the Spirit of the Risen Jesus we are to cooperate with the uncreated energies of God. Creation is not finished. It is on-going. And God calls us to share (*synergy*) in a working-with God's creative power to use our gifts and talents to transfigure this universe into the Cosmic Christ. Rather than running away from involvement in the activities of this world, such Christians move into the world, according to their talents and state of life, with enthusiasm and hope. What we add to make this world a better world in Christ Jesus, we must believe, has an eternal effect on the whole process.

Each human being in his own way is destined in God's designs to play a unique role in bringing the material world into fulfillment. Alfons Auer writes to this point:

> Henceforth man is the head and center of the cosmos. He is the living clasp by which the world of the spiritual and corporeal are fitted into one. In him the world encounters itself; in him it is present; in man it is seized into one. The world is primarily created for man so as to render possible

to man his incarnate existence. As the "extended cor-
poreality of man" the world is personally conditioned. It
must therefore follow that the God-man, in becoming the
head of the human race, also becomes the *head of the
whole material creation.*[9]

In such a vision, whatever we add by way of our
political involvements, art, thought, technology, social
and religious activities, all can serve to bring the Total
Christ to completion and to full glory. Man's greatest
creative work consists in consciously cooperating with the
creative power of God according to the mind of God to bring the universe into fulfillment. By failing to uproot sinfulness in this world, firstly, within ourselves, we obstruct
the progress of the universe. By seeking to live continually
according to the mind of God in all of our relationships,
we contribute positively to the fulfillment of God's world.

In such a vision of the distinction between the world
and God's sacred, immanent presence, the world and our
"worldly" occupations attain the fullness, by not becoming changed into something sacred, but rather by becoming
the "place" or *locus* where human beings can meet God
and bring that segment of the material world into its
fullness. Edward Schillebeeckx, O.P. writes about the profane and the sacred in the following terms:

> This means that the entire temporal dimension and the
> unabridged reality we call profane can be assumed into a
> God-related life, given that in the Son the eternal has
> presented itself personally within temporal and terrestrial
> realities. The very definition of the hypostatic union is ex-
> actly that. This also reveals the fact that thanks to Christ,
> all human history is swathed in God's love; it is assumed
> into the absolute and gratuitous presence of the mystery of

God. The worldly and the temporal remain worldly and temporal; they are not sacralized but sanctified by that presence, that is, by the God-centered life of Christ and of his faithful.[10]

It is not enough to do our work out of a vague *intention* to form somehow or other the Body of Christ. Although God is revealing Himself actively in the material world and in the daily events of our lives, we will not find Him there unless we have first discovered Him within ourselves. Having touched God immanently present as energizing love within ourselves in deep, personal prayer each day, we will be driven by the indwelling Spirit of Jesus to desire to possess Him and to be possessed by Him. In our daily work, therefore, the creative presence of Christ is to be discovered by us in everyone and everything everywhere in a cosmic *diaphany.*

The spirituality of having a pure intention to do all actions to please God was usually posited upon a separation of God and the world without a proper appreciation from God's incarnational viewpoint of the uniqueness of each material creataure to be a point of "unveiling" God's holy presence as acting love. Jesus Christ, by His resurrection, is inserted into the material world. As we "intend" to do all our works for God's greater glory and honor, we desire to discover Christ in each worldly duty. Nothing should be profane for those who know how to see Christ inside of matter.[11]

DETACHMENT

Through such consciously Christ-centered actions we strive to reach our self-fulfillment. Yet such striving cannot be successfully accomplished unless we realize in our daily lives a detachment that would prevent any of our action from being done out of any motive of self-seeking. Our human actions, especially if they bring us honors and a sense of power, can easily flatter us into thinking we have accomplished such actions by our own creative efforts. How can we maintain a delicate balance between being always a creature of God, totally dependent upon God's graces and gifts and yet freely consenting to be a co-worker with God? We can all understand the importance of being detached in our enthusiastic activities. But Christian asceticism has always taught the importance also of a positive attitude of accepting the negative elements, at least, what may seem at first to be negative until faith brings to us a different vision, that come to us as a part of our human *facticity* as being human and creatures of matter.

Jesus consistently taught the necessity that we should deny ourselves and take up our cross and follow Him (Cr.: Mt 19:38; 16:24; Mk 8:34; Lk 9:23; 14:27). He insisted that unless the grain of wheat falls into the ground and dies it will not bring forth fruit (Jn 12:24). He lived what He preached. Just as His death on the cross had meaning only as a step to the restoration of His Divine Life to humanity through His glorified body, so too the crosses, the "passive diminishments" that come to us in our daily living, either from outside agents or from our own selves, have full meaning only as a purging from us of any selfishness in order that Christ Himself may have full sway in our lives. His Heavenly Father, Jesus taught, is the vinedresser and He prunes those whom He loves in order that they may bring forth greater fruit (Jn 15:1. Cf. also: Heb 12: 5-13).

As we die to our own self-containment, we become freer to yield to the Spirit of Jesus to effect a new level of bringing Christ alive in the world. True human fulfillment and renunciation of what impedes human growth in greater love and service towards others can never be opposed. Attachment to Christ and a true service to the world cannot be attained without detachment. The cross and the resurrection go together in the Christian experience. Matter and spirit, body and soul, evil and good, are all interrelated phases of a continuous progression in true, ontological life, the life that Christ came to give us.

For such detached and purified Christians, time and space are somehow transcended and human work and suffering are brought into an "eternal now" moment of *kairos,* of God's salvific timelessness and His healing love. No longer do we love and go out and work, but now in the very moment of working we are growing in love. Teilhard de Chardin well expresses this:

> . . . the real is charged with a divine presence in the totality of its tangible layers. As the mystics knew and felt, everything becomes physically and literally lovable in God; and conversely, God can be possessed and loved in everything around us . . . every action, as soon as it is oriented toward him, takes on, without any change in itself, the psychic character of a center to center relationship. . . . of an act of love . . . At first the Christian aspired only to be able to love . . . 'while' acting. Now he is aware that he can love 'in' acting, that is to say, he can unite himself directly with the divine Center through action itself, no matter what form such action takes. In him all activity is . . . 'amorized.' . . . [12]

UNIFYING FORCE OF LOVE

As Christians, we are privileged to share God's vision of reality. We believe in His loving presence. We can hope that, as He is always faithful in His great love for us, so we also can be faithful to Him in each part of our daily life. We do fail and forget His immanent presence within us and each event. Yet hopefully we can rise and surrender ourselves in greater trust to His loving energies. Above all, His love, through the gift of His Spirit, will be a transforming power in our lives.

As we turn within and are in touch with our "inner self" in loving communication with the indwelling Trinity, we open ourselves more completely to God's transcending presence in each action of each moment. We let go of the lesser motives that *eros*, our self-centered love, formerly presented as the activating force for our work. God's *agape*-love becomes the determining factor in all that we do. Work then is love made visible. Every moment of work is an act of love that thrusts us into union with God as we work to glorify Him.

Kahlil Gibran beautifully describes, in poetic fashion, what it means to work with love:

And what is it to work with love?
It is to weave the cloth with threads
drawn from your heart, even as if your
beloved were to wear that cloth.
It is to build a house with affection, even
as if your beloved were to dwell in that house.
It is to sow seeds with tenderness and reap
the harvest with joy, even as if your
beloved were to eat the fruit.

It is to charge all things you fashion
with a breath of your own spirit,
And to know that all the blessed dead
are standing about you and watching.[13]

A coal miner, a truck driver, a housewife, a student,
an office worker, a teacher engage all day long in work
that is demanding. Such work requires concentration. Yet,
as human beings, all of these workers possess an inner
directing force, that which gives the motivation not only
for doing a given work but for determining the quality of
effort and creativity that they bring to their work. Some
workers are motivated in their work only as a means to
earn a living. Others are driven by an inner urge to excel
and find some interior satisfaction and identity at work
well done. Still other workers can see their work as done
out of love for their family or for persons they serve in
their work.

The mother, patiently working with her retarded or
her hyper-active child, knows what it means to put aside
her own self-centered motives and rise to an unselfish love
that thinks in terms of the other. Fidelity in performing
our monotonous duties through an ascending motive of
love of God and neighbor produces new levels of transcending love within us. As we, step by step, are motivated to
do our work for love of others, we continuously open
ourselves to find that God's love is being perfected as we
love others (1 Jn 4:12).

The transfiguring power of God, bathing us in His
divinizing energies of love, becomes daily a deeper experience. Our work and our moments of personal prayer
both become "places" of discovering God's loving and active presence. We become alive to an exciting world. We

live with "contuition," as Gerard Manley Hopkins, S.J. calls this simultaneous awareness of the individual creature that we are touching in our work and the dynamic presence of God as the loving Ground of Being.

THE COSMIC CHRIST

But the Christian pushes farther in faith to see what we have been stressing in this chapter. By the "game of the Resurrection" Jesus Christ has irrevocably inserted Himself into our material world. He is like a powerful *enzyme,* drawing all men who freely accept His fermenting love. He stretches out through His Body, the Church, to touch and raise us into new life. He is present in the preached Word and in His sacraments. He is present bringing the Spirit of love into every material event of our lives.

As we turn within ourselves daily in prayer and purifying reflection that heals us of our selfish love, we find Christ more easily in our material concerns. We yield our talents to His direction. We seek to live according to God's inner harmony found in each event. We become His servants as we lovingly work to serve others. It is possible by God's grace after much prayer and purification and loving service to others to live and move and act out of a conscious love for God in the most profane situations. Without detracting from our full concentration on the given tasks at hand, our work can be the environment, a *divine milieu,* in which we adore and serve God who infinitely loves and serves us in Jesus Christ and His Holy Spirit.

God is asking us at every moment to work to build the Body of His Son into its fullness. There can be no greater humanizing force in our lives than to work consciously toward this goal. For we have been created to be according to His image. We are continuously in process, through our daily lives of activities and passivities, joys and sorrows, sin and reconciliation, of being divinized into God's loving children by becoming one in His only begotten Son. As we know ourselves in the Father's eternal love, we become the extension of His Son's Body, to bring others by our love and god's love in us into that Body.

Then God's eternal plan will be completed. God will be found in all things. Divinity in all its holiness will come to rest in having finally reached the full Incarnation. But all humanity will also have reached in the end the beginning. There will be the return to the Garden of Eden and all things of the world will be in harmony with man and man will offer the whole world as a Eucharist, a perpetual thanksgiving to God.

T. S. Eliot, in his *Four Quartets,* well describes our search for our true being and our proper relationship to the rest of the world.

> We shall not cease from exploration,
> And the end of all our exploring
> Will be to arrive where we started
> And know the place for the first time.[14]

Then all of us will be brought to true life in Christ who will lead us to the Father in eternal peace and joy. The end will truly be a beginning as we continue in loving service to find God in all and all in God as St. Paul so powerfully foretells:

> Just as all men die in Adam, so all men will be brought to life in Christ; but all of them in their proper order: Christ

as the first-fruits and then, after the coming of Christ, those who belong to him. After that will come the end, when he hands over the kingdom to God the Father, having done away with every sovereignty, authority and power. For he must be king until he has put all his enemies under his feet and the last of the enemies to be destroyed is death, for everything is to be put under his feet. Though when it is said that everything is subjected, this clearly cannot include the One who subjected everything to him. And when everything is subjected to him, then the Son himself will be subject in his turn to the One who subjected all things to him, so that God may be all in all (1 Co 15: 22-28).

5

Marriage and Contemplation

Man and woman stalk this earth in feverish hunt for happiness. We seek it in money, pleasures, travel, food, sex and yet all things fail to satisfy the pain in our hearts for a happiness that would never bring us boredom, that would be imperishable, that would last forever.

After some limited experiences in life we soon learn that there can be no real happiness without love. Being alone brings bitterness, emptiness and meaninglessness to life. Love for another brings purpose to our wanderings, identity to ourselves. God made us to love: to give and accept love. He who is Love (1 Jn 4:8) has created us, not to be alone, but to receive a share in His being by loving one another. That is why God in Holy Scripture says: "It is not good that the man should be alone. I will make him a helpmate" (Gn 2:18).

God communicates His loving presence to us through all of creation. Yet He shares Himself with us more perfectly through the gifts of human beings who love us and whom we are privileged to love. God's uncreated energies of love are experienced most when we, in unselfish giving and receiving love, meet His loving presence in others. God wishes to be Himself, to become His true being for you and me by *needing* others to become the *place* where He again incarnates His great love for us. God *needs* human beings in order to become love present and experienced only because in His eternal plan He willingly constructed us as creatures to be fulfilled and happy with His life in and through human loves.

> . . . since God has loved us so much,
> we too should love one another.
> No one has ever seen God;
> but as long as we love one another
> God will live in us
> and his love will be complete in us (1 Jn 4: 11-12).

LOVE ONE ANOTHER

Christians should be the greatest lovers on earth. What others accept by an instinctual, primal reasoning, Christians accept also by faith. But their faith in God's infinite love for them empowers them to love with God's very own love. Such a faith convinces Christians of their uniqueness as persons since God creates each one in a life-long creative process to receive His personal gift of Himself in the event of each moment. More than this, we Christians believe that God's fullness of love has been shown when He gave us His only begotten Son (Jn 3: 16). Through His death on the cross and by His resurrectional presence within us and inside the whole material world, Jesus releases the Spirit of His Father, who makes us aware that we are truly God's children (Rm 8:15; Ga 4:6).

> Think of the love that the Father has lavished on us,
> by letting us be called God's children;

and that is what we are. . . .
we are already the children of God
but what we are to be in the future has not yet been revealed;
all we know is, that when it is revealed
we shall be like him
because we shall see him as he really is (1 Jn 3: 1-2).

This Jesus in God's eternal *now* is always pouring Himself out in death until the last drop of blood for love of us. With St. Paul we can live in His transcending love for each of us individually. "The life I now live in this body I live in faith: faith in the Son of God who loved me and who sacrificed himself for my sake" (Ga 2:20). Because Jesus loves us with the infinite love of the Father (Jn 15:9), Christians have the indwelling power of His Holy Spirit dwelling within them (Rm 8:9; 1 Co 3:16; 1 Co 6:19). We are to love others as He loves them. We are to love them with His power of love, His Spirit.

CHRISTIANITY NOT TRIED

But for the nearly two millenia of Christianity we do not always see that Christians, especially so-called "Christian" countries, have practised such love toward others, the essence of their faith. No doubt Christians, like non-Christians, possess their share of "sin in my members" that St. Paul speaks of (Rm 7:23). Our fallen natures resist God's grace to be loving to all human beings. And so we see ourselves bound by fears, hatred, a spirit of unforgiveness, isolation, moods of aggressive violence in thought, word and deed.

Part of the general malaise of "sin" that infects us and prevents the love of God that abides in our hearts (Rm

5:5), comes from the cultural elements that present Christianity to us in its doctrinal and devotional aspects. We have already spoken of the dichotomy that has been present especially in Western Christianity between nature and supernature, body and soul, matter and spirit. Such a separation has prevented Christians, firstly, from experiencing the full, loving presence of God in the world of nature, of matter, in the "secular" world.

Let us look at marriage in particular and see how certain historical, cultural aspects and philosophies have prevented Christian husbands and wives from becoming truly loving people to each other. Perhaps then we can see marriage through an integrated theological anthropology of man and woman as the normal "place" for husband and wife to meet the loving energies of God. As they experience God's love, very present to themselves in their mutual self-giving to each other, they progressively will become transformed into loving persons toward each other, their children, their neighbors and also the whole world. We hopefully will see that marriage should lead man and woman into a high degree of contemplation of God as love within the on-going experience of their mutual self-giving and accepting of each other's total gift.

INFLUENCE OF PLATONISM

The single factor that has most contributed to separating matter and spirit in Christianity has been the influence of Platonism on Christian thinkers.[1] The renowned classic scholar, Gilbert Murray, characterized the influence of Plato on philosophy: "The whole tendency of Greek philosophy after Plato, with some illustrious exceptions, especially among the Romanizing Stoics, was away from the outer world towards the world of the soul."[2] The spiritualism or supernaturalism that invaded Christianity and would have a great impact upon the theology of marriage owes its origin to Platonism as it became the philosophical carrier for articulating Christianity to persons of the Graeco-Roman civilization. Salvation was a special *gnosis* given to those who fled from involvement in the material world of senses to contemplate the eternal, unchangeable ideas of God.[3] Philo, the Alexandrian Jew, who platonized the Old Testament (+50 A.D.) and Plotinus (+270), the non-Christian mystic, brought a sharp dualism of soul and body, stemming from their acceptance of Plato's *soma-sema* (body-prison) doctrine, to early Christian writers who were greatly influenced by their writings.

Typical of Platonizing Christianity on a popular, piety level was the *Letter to Diognetus* of the late 2nd or 3rd century. The seeds have been sown in St. Paul's writings, watered in Justin and cultivated by Tatian and in this document there appears in full form the classical dualism of body/soul or spirit/matter:

> What the soul is in the body the Christians are in the world . . . the flesh hates the soul and wages war upon it . . . The soul loves the flesh which hates it and the limbs, and Christians love those that hate them. The soul has been shut up in the body but itself sustains the body; and Christians are confined in the world as in a prison, but themselves sustain the world. The soul dwells immortal in a mortal tabernacle and Christians sojourn among corruptible things, waiting for the incorruptibility which is in heaven.[4]

From now on Christians feel easy with such a dualism. The flesh which is equivalent to the world, to sex, to the human body, has no goal but of pursuing its base sinful pleasures, for that is its very nature. Body and world are denigrated and corrupted while the soul is immortal and is waiting for an eternal reward in Heaven, depending on its non-involvement in the things of this world. Tertullian in the Latin West (c. 195-200 fl.) and Clement, Origen, Athanasius and other Alexandrian theologians in the East bring this dualism to a polished articulation in their pastoral and speculative writings. The result, in the words of Rosemary Reuther, was that:

> both Greek and Latin Christianity remained committed to a Platonizing spirituality and eschatology that defined redemption as rejection of the body and flight of the soul from material, sensual nature.[5]

THE INFLUENCE OF ST. AUGUSTINE

St. Augustine (+430) stands as the supreme figure whose name and doctrines dominate throughout the Middle Ages from 500 A.D. to 1100 A.D. His teachings on original sin, the disobedience of the body and its basic corruptness through the fall, with his dichotomy between nature and supernature, formed the backdrop for a faulty almost anti-Christian, attitude towards the world, man's body, toward sex and marriage that has been with us in Western Christianity right up to the present day. Unable to accept his own sexuality, Augustine's doctrine shows his struggle to teach the Christian status of marriage as an honorable state meeting head-on with his Manichean training that pleasure attached to sexual intercourse was sinful except when carried out with explicit reference to a desire for procreation.

Borrowing heavily from Plotinus and his early training as a Manichee, Augustine regarded man as "crucially 'soul' fallen and immersed into an essentially alien world of sense and body."[6] Against the Manichees, he taught that marriage was good. Against the Pelagians, Augustine taught that concupiscence is evil and corrupt and any pleasure in marriage could only be tolerated in the light of a greater good, the primary end of marriage, namely, procreation. Lust is present in conjugal intercourse but it is solely procreation that makes marriage a God-pleasing institution.

John Noonan gives a devastating text from St. Augustine's writings that would impose venial sin upon all married persons, even within the limits of their marriage, who would seek solely pleasure in each other and not primarily procreation:

> It is one thing not to lie (i.e. have intercourse) except with the sole will of generating: this has no fault. It is another to seek the pleasure of the flesh in lying, although within the limits of marriage: this has venial fault. I am supposing that then, although you are not lying for the sake of procreating offspring, you are not for the sake of lust obstructing their procreation by an evil prayer or an evil deed. Those who do this, although they are called husband and wife, are not; nor do they retain any reality of marriage, but with a respectable name cover a shame. They give themselves away, indeed, when they go so far as to expose the children who are born to them against their will. . . . Sometimes this lustful cruelty or cure lust, comes to this, that they even procure poisons of sterility, and if these do not work, extinguish and destroy fetus in some

way in the womb . . . Assuredly if both husband and wife are like this, they are not married, and if they were like this from the beginning, they come together not joined in matrimony but in seduction. If both are not like this, I dare to say that either the wife is in a fashion the harlot of her husband or he is an adulterer with his own wife.[7]

Jansenism of the 17th and 18th centuries popularized Augustine's teachings and brought his teaching on marriage and sex into the ordinary parish and Christian family. We could ask whether there could have possibly been a totally different attitude toward marriage and sex if not the writings of Augustine but those of some of the more biblical oriented Greek Fathers, like Irenaeus, John Chrysostom, Maximus the Confessor, Symeon the New Theologian and Gregory Palamas would have been followed in the West. Such Christian thinkers did not have a personal history, as did St. Augustine, of Manicheanism, laden with heavy guilt for his own sexual involvements, nor did they face a dichotomizing of God's graceful activities relegated only to the supernatural sphere while nature was left sinful and corrupted. Perhaps some of the insights in this book derived basically from such Greek Fathers can be now applied to marriage. This chapter in no way is meant to be a complete treatise on marriage and sexuality. It is rather an attempt to offer to husbands and wives some insights that deal with the main theme of this book: God at the heart of matter. Instead of Augustine's dichotomizing of body and soul, cannot Christian married persons truly find God, contemplating Him at the heart of their sexual love? If Christian marriage is a sacrament, why cannot such Christians meet Jesus Christ, healing their broken sinfulness and transfiguring them into new levels of being one with each other, yet uniquely different, forming the basic membership in the Body of Christ?

THE MYSTERY OF MARRIAGE

D. H. Lawrence in his novel, *The Rainbow,* beautifully describes the mysterious quality of marriage that gives to man and woman a new level of seeing this world from a higher point of transcendence than that which the single state provides:

> It made a great difference to him, marriage. Things became so remote and of so little significance, as he knew the powerful source of his life. His eyes opened on a new universe and he wondered in thinking of his triviality before. A new calm relationship showed to him in the things he saw, in the cattle he used, the young wheat as it eddied in a wind. And each time he returned home, he went steadily expectantly, like a man who goes to a profound, unknown satisfaction.[8]

When two people marry, they submit themselves to live in a world of mystery. There is awe and wonderment. There is also an opening to one's own areas of darkness, hidden deeply within the various levels of the consciousness and the unconscious as well as to the brokenness and imperfections in the other partner. There is a call to integration as a whole person through unselfish love given at each moment of married life. Above all, for Christians, marriage is a sacrament in which husbands and wives are prayerfully, in deep faith, hope and love, to meet Jesus Christ, the Savior, who transforms by grace their sincere, loving desires into one body as He is one with His Church.

A logical analysis of marriage will never succeed in presenting its true essence. Because marriage brings together the uncreated energies of God, loving and giving Himself to the married couple, it remains always a mystery that must be approached in a prayerful reverence. Because God centers His transforming power in the material world through the risen Jesus Christ, marriage is a mysterious, sacramental encounter with and surrender to His lordship.

Marriage is a call to contemplation, a call to enter the "mystical" life. We use the term *mystical*, not to refer to that extraordinary state of the prayer-life of *mystics*, that remains closed to ordinary people. Rather, it refers in early Christian tradition to the life of God and His loving actions within the history of salvation. It is our entering into a *mystical* understanding of God's being and presence in our lives that is given by God in the darkening of our reasoning powers. It lies in the area of intuitional knowledge that is direct and immediate in our experience because it is God who does the revealing while we actively receive His revelation. We speak of the mystery of the Trinity and the Incarnation. The *mystical* life opens us up to experience God's operations in such a mystery.

Marriage is a mystery insofar as the deepest understanding of its purpose lies outside of man's logical categories. It is in a constant state of conversion, of purifying one's heart, that the mystical knowledge of marriage is given. Another way to consider marriage as mystery is to see it as a sacramental encounter with Jesus Christ.

MARRIAGE AS SACRAMENT

A sacrament is not a *thing* to be received by us. It is a mysterious action of Jesus Christ, extended through His

Church, to communicate His living and gloriously resurrected life to us. In encountering this energizing life of
Christ, which is a share in the total, Trinitarian action
toward us, we can be transformed and share in the very
life of the Trinity.

In marriage Jesus gives Himself to two people. They
can share, if they open up to His presence in their daily
lives, in His love and freeing power. They, too, can actually experience in their own self-giving to each other the very
self-giving of God to each other and to the both of them as
a one. This is a great mystery, St. Paul says.

> Give way to one another in obedience to Christ. Wives
> should regard their husbands as they regard the Lord, since
> as Christ is head of the Church and saves the whole body,
> so is a husband the head of his wife; and as the Church
> submits to Christ, so should wives to their husbands, in
> everything. Husbands should love their wives just as Christ
> loved the Church and sacrificed himself for her to make
> her holy . . . In the same way, husbands must love their
> wives as they love their own bodies; for a man to love his
> wife is for him to love himself. A man never hates his own
> body, but he feeds it and looks after it; and that is the way
> Christ treats the Church, because it is his body—and we
> are its living parts. For this reason, a man must leave his
> father and mother and be joined to his wife, and the two
> will become one body. This mystery has many implica-
> tions; but I am saying it applies to Christ and the Church.
> To sum up: you too, each one of you, must love his wife as
> he loves himself; and let every wife respect her husband
> (Ep 5: 21-33).

As Christ has given Himself to the Church, His Bride,
so the husband and the wife are to give themselves totally

and completely, permanently and exclusively to each other without any reservation or selfishness. But Christian marriage is a sacrament and is daily operative when it is entered upon and lived by Christians in faith that in all of their marital relationships they can meet Jesus Christ. They believe that in all events of their married life, Jesus Christ encounters the husband and wife and children in their love. He transforms each natural joy and suffering, doubt and fear by giving it new meaning. He is present with His resurrectional victory over sin and death.

What would be impossible on a strictly human level for two married persons to cope with and develop into a humanizing, fulfilling experience now becomes possible because they discover by faith Jesus Christ inside of the body, soul, spirit relationships. True Christian sacramentality of marriage discards an ugly separation of God from any area of married life, especially from the sexual life of husband and wife. By encountering the total self-giving of Jesus in their loving surrender to each other, they are open to find Him operating powerfully and in a transforming way in the materiality of their mutual love.

"YOUR BODIES ARE HOLY"

By a living incarnational approach to marriage, such couples can break through a pessimistic Jansenism to begin to experience God at the heart of matter. They can begin to experience themselves as individuals and as a one body in marriage in a holistic manner. No longer will they view themselves composed of two contradictory parts: body and soul. Man and woman are "ensouled" bodies and "embodied" souls.

The material body, as that of the human Christ,

becomes important. The body is the visible part of one, indivisible, unique person. We become present as a loving person with a unique identity with all our own *I-ness* in and through the body. Surely the human Jesus found the presence and divinizing action of His Father's loving Spirit in His own bodiliness as well as that of other human beings that He met and loved through His human bodiliness. If St. Paul could appeal to the Corinthians' inner dignity because their bodies were holy: "Your body, you know, is the temple of the Holy Spirit" (1 Co 6:19), how much more was this a living experience of Jesus in His body? Jesus found the Father lovingly working in nature all about Him, but He also found Him continually working in a loving manner in His own body.

St. Irenaeus of the 2nd century could say that the glory of God was a man living fully. Jesus was the most free human being that ever existed because the Spirit in Him allowed Him to find the Father, gifting Him with Himself in so many new and surprising ways. Seeing His Father in the materiality of His body, as well as that in the bodies of other human beings whom He came to love and serve, Jesus enjoyed a serenity and contentment in being *there*, localized in space and time, in touch with the energies of His loving Father who gave Himself in such materiality.

Sin sets up a physical, psychical and spiritual nervousness in us because we fail to see the loving presence of God in such relationships. We tend to exploit them, as we see in our abuses of our basic appetites for food, drink, sex, material and intellectual possessions, honors and, in a word, pride of life.

Because we are human beings and not disembodied angels, we need the body to communicate ourselves to

others. Only 30% of our comunication in human "conver-
sation" is done through spoken words. The communication of our deepest levels of uniqueness and the desire to
share that uniqueness with other persons in love come
through words of love, calling out the name of the beloved
in tender, caring accents. But there is an unlimited number
of looks, sighs, gestures, touches, embraces and, ultimately, the most primal act of sexual intercourse, that form an
essential part of human communication, especially in marriage.

Lips do not kiss but two human beings in love. Two
bodies do not copulate, but a husband and wife act out
their total, permanent commitment in love toward each
other in a body, soul, spirit intercourse. Such a conjugal
act is posited by human beings who act out their inner
psychic and spiritual oneness through two bodies becoming one. Yet when such an act is holistic and involves the
entire man and woman on all levels of their being, then
they mutually are stretching in transcendence to go beyond
the limitations of their love already attained in their consciousness.

As Christians, they can believe that it is truly God
discovered at the heart of such material communication,
activating His energizing energies to bring them into a still
greater oneness between themselves and in their rootedness
in God as their ultimate source of union and happiness.

If husband and wife looked upon their human body as
not a part separated from the soul but as the whole person
using the body as a means to communicate the Holy
Spirit's love, then physical intercourse would become a
sacred act of mystical union with God and with each other.
To oppose pleasure to procreation is to ask the wrong
question. In marital love, man and woman are gifted to

love the other somewhat as God does, in a beautiful hope of what is yet unseen but could be. The one loved has not yet experienced himself or herself as that good, noble or beautiful person, yet in the eyes of the lover he or she is already that lovable, unique person. For those who have learned to let go of their hold on their own lives and have taken the risk of hoping in the goodness of the other by being "vulnerable" and at the complete service of the one loved, great riches of contemplation begin to be experienced. A global presence of God that is distinct from the two loved ones and yet that can never be separated from them is a beginning of the joys of Heaven. It is to experience two members as forming a oneness, "bone from my bones, and flesh from my flesh" (Gn 2:23) and a larger oneness with God. It is the basic experience of Church, two members forming a oneness in Christ.

NEED FOR PURIFICATION

When we speak of love, especially in the context of marriage, we open ourselves to much confusion since love admits of many interpretations and meanings. When two young people "fall in love" and begin a life of marriage, love is seen as a "something" that mysteriously creeps up upon them and smites them, like Cupid shooting darts of love into the lovers' hearts. Much sentimentality is attached to the early stages of love that needs purification before that free, floating, whimsical spell matures into true marital love. Love is more than a physical attraction, yet in marriage the spirit in each partner grows in depth through strong, tender, joyous, gentle and passionate physical union.

Much of our modern literature deals with eroticism and confuses this with true, human, marital love Eroticism is another word for immature selfishness that uses the body of the other in intercourse as a "thing" to be possessed and used in sensuous self-seeking. Such intimacy as marriage opens each partner to share, opens them also to the unredeemed, hidden areas that come out as we see ourselves being mirrored in the openness of the other. Demands of sensitivity and fidelity not known before are called for to be made in proportion as the husband and wife receive the gift of the other. A decision must be made each time: to make self the center and thus to use the other person as an object, a mere plaything, or to die to self as the center of one's reality and seek humbly to serve the unique godliness in the other.

In marital love two people are gifted to love the other somewhat with the totality as God does. In selfishness, one or both of the partners can lose the contemplative spirit of wonder and mystery, poetry and going beyond the mere sense pleasures of the body and settle only for an ever increasing return of orgasmic pleasures. Persons who have been privileged to have entered into the very depths of the other's being in a total self-giving and self-receiving can all too easily learn how to exploit the other for his or her own self-interests.

Jesus Christ enters into the sacramental union of each marital encounter and brings His healing power to purify the husband and wife from mere self-centeredness and caprice. Each partner needs time to be alone with God in deep prayer to experience the Transcendent Other at the depths of his or her own being. As such individuals in marriage learn to love in greater consciousness of God's indwelling presence at the center of their unique being, they can progressively learn how to listen to the same God, loving with them the other partner. As prayer progressively deepens, we learn to yield more and more to God's love operating within us. So too, in marriage, as two persons learn to die to self and be toward the other in authentic, mature love, they yield also to His intense love for the two of them in each encounter.

Gone must be the forceful, nervous attacks with their secured defenses that reveal an inauthentic person, fearful to let go and love in unselfish giving to the other. Gentleness and patience and a joyful expectancy characterize each loving encounter. Purified love begets a state of constant alertness to the "otherness" of the beloved. Love becomes a listening in order to serve better, to go the other mile for the other.

One of the devastating evils of selfishness in marriage is the tendency of a husband or wife to so control the other as though he or she were a mere possession whose sole existence is to exist for the petty exploitation of the other. True marital love is total self-giving, permanent until death, and exclusive. As Christ directs His love exclusively toward His Church, so each partner must realize by God's grace operating in their marriage that their love of total surrender to each other cannot be shared with anyone else in that same manner.

Yet a sign of mature love is the ability to trust the other, to allow the loved one to have freedom to develop his other life, his or her talents according to God's gift given, and this without interference, but rather with loving support and encouragement from the other. Each partner needs a certain amount of physical, psychic and spiritual "space" to develop. Marriage should never stifle the unique growth of the individual but enhance and support it.

To this point Kahlil Gibran writes well of the delicateness in friendship not to become too possessive:

> You were born together, and together you shall be forever-
> more.
> You shall be together when the white
> wings of death scatter your days.
> Ay, you shall be together even in the
> silent memory of God.
> But let there be spaces in your togetherness.
> And let the winds of the heavens dance
> between you.
>
> Love one another, but make not a bond
> of love:
> Let it rather be a moving sea between
> the shores of your souls.
> Fill each other's cup but drink not from one cup.
> Give one another of your breaad but eat
> not from the same loaf.
> Sing and dance together and be joyous,
> but let each one of you be alone,
> even as the strings of a lute are alone
> though they quiver with the same music.
>
> Give your hearts, but not into each
> other's keeping.
> For only the hand of Life can contain
> your hearts.
> And stand together yet not too near
> together:
> For the pillars of the temple stand apart.
> And the oak tree and the cypress grow
> not in each other's shadow.[9]

A TRANSFIGURATION

Marriage is a microcosm of society and the entire universe. The cosmic Christ is present in the whole universe, effecting by the "game of the resurrection" a transformation of humanity and the sub-human cosmos into His very own Body, the Church.[10] The same risen Jesus Christ is present in the lives of two married persons, pouring into them the energies of God's love. As they open themselves to His presence in their love, they gain strength to believe in the transfiguring power of God who is infinitely beyond their own possibilities. For what is impossible to men is possible to God (Mt 19: 26; Gn 18: 14). They can believe that, out of each one's petty moods, carelessness and momentary lapses into self-centeredness, something beautiful can evolve if each partner can transcend such crosses and deaths to rise in hope to new loving, self-giving.

Jesus Christ, the Divine Physician, pours His healing love into their bodied beings, allowing them to live new lives in His love. Something of His Taboric light pierces through the monotony and banality of each day, allowing the married couple to transcend the brokenness and frailty of their human situation. Hope covers the darkness of each perplexing doubt and fear of the moment like a strong light. God's glory is seen in seeming obscurity.

> Arise, shine out, for your light has come,
> the glory of Yahweh is rising on you,
> though night still covers the earth
> and darkness the peoples (Is 60: 1-2).

CREATIVITY

Out of such mundane cares and worries, the loved ones call out in childlike trust that God will truly transform their love into new life. It is a vision of finding God in the ordinary things of married life and there to come alive with creative powers. Unsuspected energies are released in the discovery of God in their mutual love. These pour out into the tasks of everyday living, now done with a peace and joy that come from working with the uncreated energies of God in each event. "Inside," into each situation such Christians enter to bring forth their potential as alive people, working as a new creation to reconcile the world to the Father (2 Co 5: 17-18).

But the greatest creativity in the world is found when husband and wife surrender their own limitations and boundaries to burst forth in a willing act of love to want to share God's love and their being in a child of their own. When children are wanted as the peak of the mutual love of husband and wife is reached in their wanting to transcend themselves, then they touch the generosity of God in His self-giving of His life to a new human being. What father and mother have not been swept up into a true mystical experience, when they first beheld their new born baby?

To be cooperators with God in bringing forth new life is to enter deeply into the mystery of God's great, creative love for us. It hurls parents into a dizzying wonderment that touches the center of God's active love and makes Him truly felt, perhaps for the first time in their lives, as a loving, involved God who is not far away. " . . . since it is in him that we live and move and exist" (Ac 17: 28).

Man and woman in their children extend their love for

each other and for God and the world. Their love is not only immortalized in their concrete children but their love grows as it is multiplied in their matured sons and daughters, loving as their parents loved to extend still further this love into eternity. Bearing offspring is God's blessing on their conjugal love and it reaps a hundred-fold that selfish people in marriage may never experience because to love truly is to live fully our Baptism.

DEATH UNTO GLORY

And that Baptism is a true death to all that impedes building a community of persons in a loving oneness to rise to a new sharing in God's glory. The fruit of all Christian, sacramental life is a state of living the Eucharist of Jesus Christ toward each other within the married family. It is a firm commitment forever, in all circumstances, to reverence and serve the other or others in the family. The law that Jesus so insistently taught and, more so, lived out in His Person is that of the seed falling into the earth and dying. Only in such a death can new life, more abundantly come forth (Jn 12:24).

Love, therefore, is a way of contemplating each person with something of God's vision. It is to go beyond the externals to touch the uniqueness in the other that ultimately comes from God's unique love for that individual. It is caring for the other in an habitual attitude of concern. It is not only telling the other often of one's love for the other, but, above all, it is acting always out of the motive of what is good for the other. It is a listening to see how much more of loving service one can perform to bring the other greater happiness.

In the stage play, *The Subject Was Roses,* a father hears these words from his child:

> There was a dream I used to have about you and I . . . . It was always the same . . . I'd be told that you were dead and I'd run crying into the street . . . Someone would stop me and ask why I was crying and I'd say, "My father's dead and he never said he loved me."[11]

When husband and wife care for each other and think only in terms of loving service toward the other, this respect for the otherness of the one loved flows out to the children. Such a loving family will radiate the love of God toward the uniqueness reverenced in their neighbors. Such a love, rooted in God's very own love for each of His children, will spread out in an openness to serve all human beings, whoever or wherever they may be.

A LOVING CHURCH—THE BODY OF CHRIST

Such a gift of presence grows as it is experienced and given away to all who pass by. It blossoms forth, always bringing forth new life. It is a small candle that becomes a torch, lighting the way through darkness to life. Married man and woman have been touched by God. In their love for each other they have truly touched God. As they extend this love toward others, they contemplate the same God in such relationships.

The Holy Spirit of Jesus Risen brings them from their conjugal love to a universal love toward all human beings. They have contemplated God communicating His very own life to them as they opened themselves in their total body, soul, spirit relationships. They go forth from their family to contemplate the same Trinity communicating His life to others in and through their love. They *see* the Body of Christ forming within the context of His members in whom He lives through His Holy Spirit. They experience the presence of Jesus as Word preached and sacraments received, above all, as His love in individual persons uniting all members into one Body. In that Body, Jesus still lovingly touches this world to raise it to a transfigured level of fulfillment.

The mystery of Jesus loving His Bride, the Church, contains the microcosm and the macrocosm. Husband and wife contemplate the risen Jesus, releasing His Spirit of love within their hearts, to bind them irrevocably and exclusively into a oneness, two bodied beings now being made more and more one in Christ. In all of their outgoing social relationships toward others they contemplate the same Jesus, by the power of His Spirit, bringing all men and women into one Body (Ep 4:4).

Stripped of all selfishness in their conjugal love, such purified Christians can contemplate the presence of Jesus, in the sacredness of matter. They can "inscape" into the material world and there be co-creators of new life in the universe.

CONTEMPLATIVES IN THE WORLD

As God calls His people back to the vision revealed in the Old and New Testaments of Himself as a loving God, actively involved in the materiality of this world to give us a share in His divine life, Christians can break through a false separation of matter and spirit. God is calling married people to realize that all His children are to become holy and perfect as He is.

. . . be holy in all you do, since it is the Holy One who has
called you, and scripture says: Be holy, for I am holy (1 P
1: 15-16).

Being perfect or holy is a continuous progress in love.
It is of obligation on all of us, regardless of our state of
life. The Vatican Council II *Constitution on the Church*
declares this universal call to sanctity: "In the Church not
everyone marches along the same path, yet all are called to
sanctity and have obtained an equal privilege of faith
through the justice of God."[12] It goes on to affirm that all
the laity have the exalted duty of working for the ever
greater spread of the divine plan of salvation to all men
over all the earth.[13]

To give the love of God to others by our love for them
is first to experience profoundly God's deep, personal love
for us. Married men and women are called by God daily to
experience that love in intimate moments alone and
together in prayer before God. Contemplative prayer
demands time to be spent leisurely listening to God.
Through the Holy Spirit who alone teaches all Christians
how to pray, husbands and wives will progressively come
to *know* the depths of the uncreated love of the Trinity.
They will be able to comprehend with all the saints the
breadth, length, depth and height of the love of Christ that
surpasses all other human knowledge (Ep 3: 18-19).

Their very own sexual love through their bodiliness
will no longer be an obstacle but a beautiful, incarnational
point to meet the freshly nascent energizing love of God at
the heart of their embodied love. God calls them to contemplate His transforming love in their mutual, total self-
giving to each other. Such contemplation is a transformation into a channel of love for the whole material world.

To the degree that such married couples have contemplated God in their conjugal love, to that degree will they actively be able to serve God in a return of love. True contemplation is measured by our love for others in humble service. Such contemplatives discover God in all things and all things in God. Yet they discover the secret that contemplative husbands and wives should continually experience. In the surrender toward any loving union, one discovers his or her own unique personhood. We should no longer speak of whether marriage is an obstacle to sanctity. Let us see in God's eternal design that marriage is a privilege where two people learn progressively to fall in love with each other and with God simultaneously. It is the normal school to form contemplatives who will adore God in His material world and, by loving service, they will co-create this world into the very Body of Christ.

> May they all be one.
> Father, may they be one in us,
> as you are in me and I am in you,
> so that the world may believe it was you who sent me.
> I have given them the glory you gave to me,
> that they may be one as we are one.
> With me in them and you in me,
> may they be so completely one
> that the world will realise that it was you who sent me
> and that I have loved them as much as you loved me
>   (Jn 17: 21-23).

6

To Be Eucharist

What makes Christianity unique among all other religions is the mystery of the Incarnation. Not only non-Christians but also many who believe themselves to be true Christians find it difficult to embrace the paradox that God so loves the human race that He became irrevocably a part of humanity when His only begotten Son "became flesh and dwelt among us" (Jn 1:14).

Throughout history certain people have opted more for the divinity in the person of Jesus Christ to the weakening or complete denial that He was truly human. This was at the basis of Docetism and Monophysitism, two heresies that in substance denied that God would have anything to do with matter.

Other groups who called themselves Christians claimed that Jesus was totally human and gradually God "adopted" Him and His divine Son. Such *adoptionists* were called Arians after their leader, Arius, who denied that Christ was the pre-existent Word of God. For such, God was all too divine and in utter transcendence could never condescend to have a part with a finite world. In a way, the same error is at the basis of both heresies, namely, that God is single, holy, perfect and could never become immersed in matter that is multiple, profane and imperfect.

MODERN CHRISTOLOGIES

History continually repeats itself. Sometimes theologians fashion new expressions of Christology because they seek to offset a former emphasis that laid too much stress on one or other aspect of the paradoxical mystery of the Incarnation. Their attempts at new articulations stem from the way they understand God or man. They seek to correct a former exaggeration, but all too often they too fall into an equal exaggeration.

Because Christian theologians for many centuries stressed the divinity of Jesus, some modern theologians seek now to accentuate His humanity. They gather their ideas about Jesus from the Gospel narratives. They start "from below." In such a view, Jesus is a man, born as all of us huma beings. He grows and develops through life experiences as we do and gradually He comes to a realization that He is the Son of God. In such a view, Jesus cannot be considered the pre-existent Son of God.[1]

THE CHURCH

As Christians conceive Jesus Christ, so they develop and live out a doctrine of the Church. If Jesus is conceived of as being more divine than human, the Church becomes a disincarnated body, fleeing from world involvement. If Jesus is seen as more human than divine the Church develops as a humanistic agency, a do-gooder institution that can hardly be discerned as any different from a civil social organization.

Today both the Christology and the image of the Church are undergoing an overhauling by certain modern thinkers. In both cases the approach is "from below." Whether "from below" or "from above," both approaches are attempts at objectivizing one element over another, to the complete loss of the mystery. In the early Church Jesus Christ was not scrutinized by human minds, dissected into parts to the destruction of the whole Person. The Church was a living body of people baptized into the Trinitarian life. These Christians met together in a spirit of humble contemplation and adoration to celebrate God's revelation of love in history, especially in the mystery of the Incarnation, death and Resurrection of Jesus Christ, the only begotten Son of God.

As a community in prayer, they not only heard the Word preached but they literally received the living Word, God-Man, Jesus Christ, in the Eucharist. They entered into the act of the Eucharist, the Liturgy (the prayer of the faithful), to become *offerers* of Jesus Christ to God and to become those *offered* in Jesus Christ.[2] Although being many, they came together that in the fellowship (*koinonia*) of the Holy Spirit, they might become one Body, one faith in Christ (Ep 4:4).

One of the earliest Eucharistic texts, the *Didache,* formulates the Christian community's prayer:

> As this broken bread was scattered upon the hills and was gathered together and made one, so let thy Church be gathered together into thy kingdom from the end of the earth . . .[3]

Our Christian faith finds its climax in the Eucharist. In the preaching of the Word of God, our faith in God's infinite love for mankind is built up by pondering prayerfully some aspect of Jesus' teaching or personality. Our faith reaches its peak in the Eucharist as we, a praying, adoring community, surrender to the mysterious, transforming action of the Trinity, Father, Son and Holy Spirit.

In the Eucharist we touch the base of all reality, the Holy Trinity. Here are concentrated the uncreated, loving energies of God. God's fullness of love moves towards us to transform us into His loving children.

A TRANSFORMING WORD

When theologians objectivize Jesus Christ by their rational powers, they may be saying some partial truth. Likewise, when we receive Jesus Christ in the Eucharist and objectivize Him outside of the Trinity, we too become objectivized and separated from the Trinitarian action upon the total Body of Christ, the Church.

In Hebrew, *dabar* means *word*. It partakes of a certain conceptualized content that can be understood and grasped by our human minds. But it also and above all possesses a dynamic, transforming power that engulfs those who receive the Word with surrendering love. In this Word—Jesus Christ—is the fullness of divinity. To His transforming presence by the power of His Spirit given to us in the Eucharist, we are to give ourselves in order to be made Eucharist for the world. St. Paul writes:

> You must live your whole life according to the Christ you have received—Jesus the Lord; you must be rooted in him and built on him and held firm by the faith you have been

taught, and full of thanksgiving . . . In his body lives the fullness of divinity, and in him you too find your own fulfilment, in the one who is the head of every Sovereignty and Power (Col 2: 6-9).

How many times we have been privileged to receive the Holy Eucharist! But because we were busy "talking" to an objectivized Jesus, whether we conceived of Him as more divine than human or vice versa, we failed to yield to His transforming power. Did we open ourselves to His divinizing power, the indwelling Holy Spirit? The fact that we have eaten the Bread of eternal Life and left the Church-community to act as dead bread to the hungry around us reveals how little of Jesus' power we allowed to transform us. How can we so often partake of Divine Fire and yet not cast the same Fire upon the earth?

We believe that we receive God's concentrated love in Jesus Christ as He always in the *now* moment of the Eucharist gives Himself as sacrament and sacrifice to us. Yet we go forth to show a lack of that love, of being a continued extension of the sacrament and sacrifice of Jesus to all that we meet.

A BLESSING TO OTHERS

In the Last Supper when Jesus first gave Himself to His Church-community as Eucharist, He gave a blessing. A blessing (in Hebrew *berakah*) in the Old Testament was a creative act, whether given by God to His people or to an individual or by an individual human person to another. God blesses His creation, all living creatures, above all, man, and empowers man to be a similar creative blessing for all creatures given to man by God. God blesses Noah after the flood and also Abraham and restores His covenant through those blessings with the human race.

Monika Hellwig describes the importance of a Jewish blessing:

> A blessing is a creative act; it brings something new into existence. It gives an increase of life and of the inheritance that God has bestowed upon his creatures. But a blessing is always expected to make the one who receives it the source of blessing for others; it is not expected to come to rest in its recipient and to end there.[4]

At the Last Supper, Jesus prays at least parts of the great 18 *Tefillah* blessings which made up the *berakoth* blessings of the Synagogue service and that of meals. We catch something of His blessings in St. John's record of the priestly prayer of Christ (Jn 17: 1-26). He glorifies the Father. He offers to Him thanksgiving and a prayer of praise and confession that directs all things to the Father as beginning and end, the source of all blessings. Centered upon His Heavenly Father, Jesus gives His blessing to His Disciples.

It is here that we enter into the peak of God's uncreated energies of love as imaged by Jesus for His followers. St. John the Evangelist prefaces the love action (Eucharist) of Jesus on behalf of His Disciples by these words:

> . . . and Jesus knew that the hour had come for him to pass from this world to the Father. He had always loved those who were his in the world, but now he showed how perfect his love was (Jn 13:1).

His hour of the Passover was approaching when Jesus would freely give Himself back to the Father in obedience

unto death for our sake, so that we, partaking of the Lamb
of God, as our food and drink, might be transformed by
the gift of Himself for us. In symbolic form of bread and
wine Jesus surrenders Himself completely to His Father
out of love for His followers, including us and all believers
down through the centuries. The bread and the wine are
His flesh and blood to be consumed by His loved ones. He
seals His gift by the words: "Do this as a memorial of me"
(Lk 22:19). His prayer is an effective prayer but not one
that merely asks His followers to return psychologically to
the Last Supper and merely remember His great love. It is
a prayer of perpetual effectiveness because Jesus is pledging His fidelity to be present as loving sacrifice whenever
this ritual is enacted.[5]

ONENESS IN THE BODY OF CHRIST

We can believe that the Disciples of Jesus were lifted
up to new heights of insight and of loving, both towards
Jesus and towards one another and the whole world. They
could not understand fully what was happening. But one
thing must have been clearer to them that evening than at
the other meals that they had eaten with Jesus, their
Master. The meaning of His full gift of Himself on their
behalf, as symbolized in the Eucharist that they had just
partaken of, could not have been known to them since the
meaning of the cross still was hidden from them. Yet they
must have grasped His immense, torrential love for them
as a body and as unique individuals. His love must have
poured over them in a new, energizing manner, lifting
them into that powerful stream of love. Only the release of
the Holy Sprit would enlighten their minds to understand
and to live in the power of that love.

A new bond of unity bound each disciple to the other

and to the whole group. They must have been aware of their sinfulness and unworthiness that purified them and opened their hearts to want, at least, to wash the feet of one another in loving, humble service.

We do not receive the Eucharist in order to speak pious sentiments to Jesus, as an object of our adoration. In the Eucharist we too, like the first Disciples of Jesus, are swept up into the loving energies of Jesus for one another, for His whole Body. Through the Eucharist, we break out in faith to put on the total mind of the Father, Son and Holy Spirit. In the microcosmic communion with the transfigured Bread and Wine, we are brought into a deeper faith to a cosmic communion, first with the Body of Christ, with those members living by faith in Jesus as Lord. There is no receiving the Body of Christ unless we receive the whole Church and thisincludes an openness of our part to love and serve the whole of humanity.

St. Paul gives us the fruit of the Eucharist:

> Bear with one another charitably, in complete selflessness, gentleness and patience. Do all you can to preserve the unity of the Spirit by the peace that binds you together. There is one Body, one Spirit just as you were all called into one and the same hope when you were called (Ep 4: 2-3).

More specifically, St. Paul writes: "The fact that there is only one loaf means that, though there are many of us, we form a single body, because we all have a share in this one loaf" (1 Co 19: 17). But should any who receive of the Body and Blood of Jesus and offend in charity their neighbors, they do not recognize the Body of Christ by failing to recognize His members and thus " . . . a person who eats and drinks without recognizing the body is eating and drinking his own condemnation" (1 Co 11: 29).

In Chapters 12 and 13 of his first epistle to the Corinthians, St. Paul highlights the gifts of the Holy Spirit that build up the Body of Christ. Each member is to use his gift or gifts to serve the whole Body. If one part hurts, the healthy parts come to the aid of the injured member. But the greatest gift and fruit of the Sprit given especially in the Eucharist is that of love. Such love is toward others as Jesus, the image of the love of the Father, was always toward others in loving service. It is always patient and kind, never jealous, never boastful or conceited, never rude or selfish. It does not take offense and is not resentful. It takes no pleasure in other people's sins but delights in the truth. It is always ready to excuse, to trust, to hope and to endure whatever comes (1 Co 13: 4-6).

Teilhard de Chardin beautifully describes this fruit of love that comes to us in the Eucharist:

> The gift you ask of me for these brothers of mine—the only gift my heart can give them—is not the overflowing tenderness of those special, preferential loves which you implant in our lives as the most powerful created agent of our inward growth: it is something less tender but just as real and of even greater strength. Your will is that, with the help of your Eucharist, between men and my brother-men there should be revealed that basic attraction (already dimly felt in every love once it becomes strong) which mystically transforms the myriads of rational creatures into (as it were) a single monad in you, Christ Jesus.[6]

JESUS PRESENT IN THE CHURCH COMMUNITY

The Eucharist is a sign, not only of our union with Jesus Christ and the Heavenly Father by the illumination of the Spirit of love, but, above all, of our union or our desire to lovingly work towards union with all mankind. We see this truth taught by St. Luke in his narrative of the two disciples meeting the Risen Jesus on the road to Emmaus. Jesus patiently explained the texts from Scripture that taught the necessity of the Messiah's suffering in order to enter into glory.

Although Jesus was physically present to them, nevertheless, their eyes were kept from recognizing Him because they were still judging, not by faith within th context of the Word's presence and action to the community of God's people, but by the physical side of the Word. It was only in the "breaking of the bread" that their eyes were opened to recognize Jesus present to them. Luke and the early Church-community are saying that there is a new presence of the Risen Jesus that goes beyond His physical presence. The Word of God is present and recognized as such, not by seeing Him, but by hearing the Christian community that gathers together through Jesus' Spirit and that speaks that Word in continuity with God's revelation in Tradition, both of the Old and New Covenant. There can be no contact with the glorious, risen Jesus except in His Body, the Church, nor can there be receiving of His eucharistic Body except in that Church, the Body of Christ, that in space and time now makes Him present to us.[7]

But what precisely makes a Church-community a praying one? True community, according to Bernard Lonergan, is the "achievement of a common meaning." It is not fashioned by whim of circumstance nor does it arise simply from the accidents of geographical nearness. A true community is realized by a centration of wills in love, loyalty and faith upon a common vision.

The common ideal of a Church-community is its point

of active convergence of individual human beings who through faith in the indwelling presence of the Risen Jesus, under the impulse of the Holy Spirit, are on their way toward the Heavenly Father. It is an ideal that embraces all of humanity, eventually united around Christ. He is the Head and we are His members. His divine life courses through us. His Spirit binds us into a unanimity of faith, worship and singbleness of purpose. The goal is a distant one, at least in its fuller realization. Mankind is torn now by division and large segments of it still are oblivious that salvation has come to it in Christ.

Yet in the Church men and women are already being gathered together around Christ by the Spirit and in the Church the witness is already being given that salvation is now being realized. Members of such a Church-community seek to signify and to witness, both by *being* and by *doing* that men are one in Christ Jesus. As the early Christian community described itself in Acts: "There was one heart and one soul in all the company of believers" (Ac 4:32).

Such is the Christian ideal and how exacting it is! Only the force of God's Word and the power of the Spirit can blend indocile hearts and wills into this oneness in Christ. In communion with Him, especially in a life of eucharistic communion, the community is grafted on to the Paschal mystery. In it, it entrusts its weaknesses and sinfulness to the strength of Jesus the Healer. The elements of death and division in it are transmuted into factors of life and unity. Love, the gift of the Spirit (Rm 5: 5), transforms hearts and effects communion among them at the deep level of faith.. Energized by the oneness thus produced, love then issues forth into dynamic, apostolic service keyed to respond to contemporary needs. Thus our dedication to these needs springs out of the heart of our community with one another and our oneness with another is woven out of our involvement in a common purpose.

A Christian community exists only where charity and liberty flourish; where union is fostered and harmony is perfected. This union is not the residue after all differences have been removed. It is a harmonious synthesis, a confrontation of differences, but an integration of all those concerned, for the sake of common purpose. It is a synthesis of one another in love stemming from the mutual respect for otherness, rooted in the common Fatherhood of all God's children in Christ Jesus.

What makes the Church-community unique over all other communities is the common faith, hope and love received in Baptism that allow each member to become incorporated into this community that is truly the very Body of the Risen Lord Jesus. The Resurrection for the first Christians was not merely a historical event that allowed Jesus in His Resurrection and in His presence, now in a wonderful new dispensation of grace, whereby the Holy Trinity would now live within the Christian members.

This community into the Body of Christ is a gift given by God's Spirit. We read how this early Church-community was formed:

> These remained faithful to the teaching of the apostles, to the brotherhood, to the breaking of bread and to the prayers. The many miracles and signs worked through the apostles made a deep impression on everyone. The faithful all lived together and owned everything in common; they sold their goods and possessions and shared out the proceeds among themselves according to what each one needed. They went as a body to the Temple every day but met in

their houses for the breaking of bread; they shared their food gladly and generously; they praised God and were looked up to by everyone. Day by day the Lord added to their community those destined to be saved. (Ac 2: 42-47).

A PRAYING COMMUNITY

Prayer, as the lifting of the mind and heart to God in response to His Word, directing and carrying the whole of our lives to God as a living liturgy, is of the essence of the Christian existence. Only the individual person can allow himself to be lifted up in mind and heart to God and to receive God's personal love and to return that love by a self-surrender. Hence there can be no true community prayer-life without deep personal prayer. The movement inwardly, as Jesus taught His Disciples, is to meet the Father within the deep recesses of our being and there to adore Him in silence and awe (Mt 6:6). Every Christian is destined to grow in the service of building up the Kingdom of God, the *koinonia;* hence one's personal prayer can never end with himself alone, but always it must be a movement outwardly towards others, to build the community of many in a oneness of God's life within all, uniting all in a new creation.

Such individual prayer that is both necessary in solitude and in community is man and woman standing outside of themselves before their God, looking at God with the totality of their being and recognizing Him as their source of total existence. It is an offer in praise and worship of one's complete self in return for the gift of total being received from God. Such personal prayer should lead us more and more into this mysterious knowledge and experience of God as the Ground of our being. This cannot be seized by force of our intellects but it is an intuition given to the humble of heart by God.

The movement in personal prayer is from the discursive prayer of reasoning to an ever greater movement in deeper faith, more receptivity, through purification of our hearts, into an infused contemplation where we see all things in God's light. Such personal prayer is fed by communal prayer and communal prayer grows richer in understanding and love for all mankind precisely through the increase of intense personal prayer.

St. Paul describes the inter-relation of a Spirit-filled community, liturgical communal prayer and the continuing private, personal prayer:

> Sing the words and tunes of the paslms and hymns when you are together, and go on singing and chanting to the Lord in your hearts, so that always and everywhere you are giving thanks to God who is our Father in the name of our Lord Jesus Christ (Ep 5: 19-20).

St. Peter calls the Christians to realize their dignity:

> But you are a chosen race, a royal priesthod, a consecrated nation, a people set apart to sing the praises of God who called you out of the darkness into his wonderful light (1 P 2:9).

The main purpose of this Church-community, therefore, is to worship and praise God. Any apostolic activity flows from the praise of God and the experience of our common Father over us all. It is the fruition of an experience in personal and communal prayer of being saved by Christ Jesus and hence wanting to bring this same new life to others throughout the entire world.

THE PRAYER OF THE EUCHARIST

In Church-community there are various forms of prayer. Some forms are unstructured and spontaneous, in small, informal groups that represent the Church where two or three gather in Christ's name. Other forms are more structured and liturgical. The word *liturgy* comes from the Greek words, *leitos,* meaning that it pertains to the people, and *ergon,* meaning work. It is, therefore, a work done for the people. In the spiritual sense, liturgy is the vehicle for prayer and the form of the worshipping community. It is a lived experience rooted in the living tradition, both oral and written.

Liturgy is essentially worship by a community and takes on many forms. It is prayer in petition, propitiation, adoration and thanksgiving. It is action in its processions, bodily movements and gestures. But most importantly, it is only properly a liturgy when it is an activity of the community in which God is the Center. Man is the recipient of this indwelling God and in such a community God forms the Church, the Body of Christ. The Church becomes the Body through which God's work is extended, namely, His adoration by the community and the sanctification of the community through the sanctification of the individual members of it. In its entirety it is a prayerful commemoration of our redemption through the death and resurrection of Jesus Christ. The liturgy is the sacred time when the Church realizes itself. It is the realization of the life of the Church for which it exists: to praise and glorify God for the gifts of life and salvation we have received.

The Constitution on the Liturgy of Vatican Council II insists that the liturgy is the peak action of the Church:

Nevertheless the liturgy is the summit toward which the activity of the Church is directed; at the same time it is the foundation from which all her power flows. For the goal of apostolic works is that all who are made sons of God by faith and baptism should come together to praise God in the midst of His Church, to take part in her sacrifice, and to eat the Lord's supper.[8]

OPENNESS TO THE WORLD

It is almost a cliche to say that we live the way we pray and we pray the way we live. The quality of our prayer-life is the test of the worth of the rest of our life. The rest of our life, outside of our personal and communal prayer, reveals the quality of that prayer. Prayer is not finished until it is lived. The Eucharist is the Bread of Life to be shared with others. Have we really lifted our hearts to God if we have not offered Him our whole being, with our whole set of relationships to other people who touch us and whom we touch in daily life? Of what avail is our offering in the community's liturgy if it is not completed in the offering in our living?

Prayer is perfect in doing, in living according to the Father's salvific will. Prayer can never be abstract or separated from our daily living. If it is true prayer, it must spring from our life and be expressed and completed in life. St. Paul exhorts us: " . . . and worship him, I beg you, in a way that is worthy of thinking beings, by offering your living bodies as a holy sacrifice, truly pleasing to God" (Rm 12:1). The problem of how to pray and how to live is really the same problem. Personal holiness, rooted in one's intimate communion with God, grows in love's interpersonal relations for the love of God needs to be expressed in the love of the neighbor.

It was H.A. Reinhold who stirred up the Christian conscience in America to see that justice and charity cannot be excluded. The liturgy, carried out to perfection exteriorly, will be a tinkling cymbal in the ears of God unless the ones who celebrate it continue to glory in the same Lord in the economic, social, political and cultural fields. The intense participation of community prayer and sharing in the Body of Christ in the Eucharist are measured by the degree of our sharing ourselves with each other before the Father of us all.

For this reason Max Delespesse can write:

> The sharing of what they have is possible because they share what they are . . . Let us recall now only that a sharing on the level of persons precedes a sharing of things and this can come about only because things are extensions of people. It was because the first Christians were of one heart and soul that they pooled their material goods for the benefit of all.[9]

The early Christians call us back to a basic Christian view that can be accepted and understood by persons who pray. In today's society more stress is placed on the private ownership of property and wealth, but in the 4th and 5th century of the Holy Fathers, those spiritual giants of God who deeply prayed out the message of the Gospel and sought to live it in their ascetical life, material possessions were essentially common property belonging to all mankind. Their deep prayer made them realize the *koinonia,* the community of all mankind under one loving Heavenly Father. God had bequeathed His creation and all creatures, not to a few individuals but to all mankind.

Today any serious Christian, who prays deeply in the heart in his own personal, solitary prayer and in liturgical community, is impelled to be concerned with the rampant poverty throughout the world. He cannot muffle his ears and block out the cries of his suffering brothers and sisters wherever they may be in the world, victims of oppression, wars or natural calamities.

The important element in true, authentic prayer is that all of us will constantly be thrust forth into our immediate communities and there witness to the Gospel values by fighting all social injustices, according to our talents and charisms. A person of deep prayer shares theinfinite compassion and love of God, who gradually by His Holy Spirit effects a divinizing process in him. He does not distinguish as Jesus also did not between this or that need, bodily, psychical or spiritual. His self-giving goes out simply toward a total individual, his very own brother and sister in Christ. It is this or that needy person in all his or her own particularity and individuality whom he seeks lovingly to serve.

WHATSOEVER YOU DO TO THE LEAST . . .

We can easily receive the message of Jesus, even receive His Body and Blood, and not let it affect us deeply in our human relationships toward others, if that message is received only as a concept, something in the "head." His message must be received in a *metanoia,* a conversion of heart. We need to see how unfree we are to love the whole world and to cry out constantly with hope that Jesus can set us free to live His eucharistic presence to others.

That message, as Chapter 6 of St. Luke's Gospel shows us, transforms us into loving Christians who forgive our enemies, turn the other cheek and insist on going another mile. *More* is the only measure of how much to give to others, not merely justice. Self-defense and secured power yield easily in the light of others' needs. The only question is: what does my brother or sister need?

To me it is incongruous that a dynamic Christian, before so many needy orphans, widows, elderly and poor, hungry and illiterate throughout the world, could remain a very wealthy person. The judgment of Jesus would sting such a person who stores up money in banks for security when the hungry and the sick cry out for comforting (Mt 25). The rebuke of St. James would sift the false, wealthy pseudo-Christians from the true Christians, poor in spirit and rich in sharing love:

> Take the case, my brothers, of someone who has never done a single good act but claims that he has faith. Will that faith save him? If one of the brothers or one of the sisters is in need of clothes and has not enough food to live on, and one of you says to them, 'I wish you well; keep yourself warm and eat plenty,' without giving them these bare necessities of life, then what good is that? Faith is like that: if good works do not go with it, it is quite dead (Ja 2: 14-16).

One's life becomes progressively more simple and uncluttered with attachment to riches, possessions, expensive clothing, food and drink, honors and positions of power. Because such a Christian has been freed by Jesus who comes as the Bread of Life, he can afford to fight for human rights wherever they are being violated. Such a Christian is guided by God's values. He is, therefore, ready:

... to listen to religious leaders for their superior knowledge of the scriptures and traditions, but not to surrender one's conscience to them or follow themin infidelities and compromises; to scrutinize all laws and dispositions of the civil authority by the law of God and be ready at all times for civil disobedience; to be prepared to find oneself constantly in a persecuted, despised and ridiculed minority, and to accept this as the necessary stance to accomplish the redemption that Jesus offers.[10]

THE HEART OF CHRIST

When we receive the Body and Blood of Jesus Christ in the Eucharist, we are invited to enter into His heart, the heart or in-depth consciousness that He revealed in the scriptural text from St. John's Last Supper discourse. We see the heart of Christ turned totally towards His Heavenly Father in adoration and praise.

> Father, the hour has come:
> glorify your Son
> so that your Son may glorify you;
> . . . I have glorified you on earth
> and finished the work that you gave me to do.
> . . . I have made your name known
> to the men you took from the world to give me.
> . . . I have known you,
> and these have known
> that you have sent me (Jn 17: 1-4, 6, 25).

He shows a heart, both in the Last Supper and in the Garden of Gethsemane, that is total gift back to the Father who has given Himself totally to His Son. He seeks only to do the will of His Father, not His own (Lk 22:43). He pours out a heart full of thanksgiving and praise to the Father. He prays also for His beloved Disciples that they may become one as He and the Father are one.

The heart of Christ is also turned toward a broken, suffering world and so He prays for that world to His Father. He looks with love upon His chosen Apostles and loves each one in all his frailty and sinfulness. They would be the pillars of His Church. He would extend His healing love through their hands and mouths to bring salvation to the whole world. He gives Himself in that first Eucharist, and in every one that is done as a memorial of it, for the remission of sins of a world that is groaning in travail. ". . . this is my blood, the blood of the covenant, which is to be poured out for many for the forgiveness of sins" (Mt 26:28).

He is ready to give His life unto the last drop of blood so that human beings may be reconciled to His Father and come into the unity of His very own Body and thus have life everlasting. This is His moment of pure love for a suffering world. It is caught forever in an eternal *now*.

His heart is turned also toward the cross of the next day. He loves us unto death. That will be the "hour" of His passing-over from His own self-containment to become the fully realized expression, the living Word of God, of His infinite love for mankind. There can be no glory given to Jesus unless He becomes obedient to His Father, unto the death of the cross (Ph 2:10). He cannot be risen except that He suffers and dies.

PUT ON THE MIND OF CHRIST

When we receive the eucharistic Christ, we are to be transformed interiorly: "Be renewed in the spirit of your mind" (Ep 4:23). There must be an inner revolution of the way we perceive God, ourselves and others.

> Do not model yourselves on the behavior of the world around you, but let your behavior change, modelled by your new mind. This is the only way to discover the will of God and know what is good, what it is that God wants, what is the perfect thing to do (Rm 12:2).

By not objectivizing the Eucharist, but by opening ourselves to the transforming power of Jesus Christ, the Eucharist will allow us, both within the context of the sacred action of the liturgy and the context of our daily living, to stand first in union with Jesus Christ before the Heavenly Father and praise Him. By praising and blessing the Father, we open ourselves at all times to His transforming blessing that He breathes upon us to make us a true, effective blessing to all whom we meet.

We put on the mind of Christ in the Eucharist when we face with Him a broken, suffering world. We share the caring love of Jesus for each suffering person we meet. We present in intercessory prayer first our loved ones and those physically close to us whose needs are known to us in the human situation in which God has placed us. Pain gnaws at our hearts as we suffer the pain of the heart of Christ not to be able to do more for the poor and afflicted in all parts of the world. We suffer in our own inadequacies that do not allow us to know what we can effectively do to alleviate the physical and moral evils rampant in the world.

As we experience Jesus, not only praying for us individually in the Eucharist, but also washing our feet, binding up our wounds, dying for love of us, so we also will want to face a broken, suffering world. We will willingly move and more each day live for others in unselfish service to the first persons who enter into our lives and look for our love.

Jesus is asking us to become Eucharist for the hungry of the world. He wishes to be present to others in their suffering needs, to become localized again in the darkness of a world that will never comprehend His light unless we bring Him there. To look on the faces of suffering man and woman is to look on the face of *the* Son of Man, Jesus Christ. The image is defaced, marred, spit upon, beaten. Its beauty can be restored only by the Bread of Life. And as the Apostles took the five loaves and few fishes and found them multiplied with food left over as they fed the multitude of 5,000, so we bring the Eucharist of Jesus Christ, the nourishment to feed the world.

As they are fed by our Christ-love, they truly turn also into the very Body of Christ. Then they can distribute the Bread of Love to others and build up the Body, the Church, until the whole of humanity will become Eucharist, a blessing to the Father and a transforming blessing to each other.

TILTED TOWARD THE CROSS

But we cannot be Bread broken unless, in receiving the Eucharist, we, like Jesus, face the cross. Jesus loved, served and healed us only because He was ready to forget Himself and live for us. There can be no true love, no true Eucharist, without this readiness to go to the cross and embrace death to oneself.

Especially today in our affluent age, we must daily receive in the Eucharist the strength of Jesus to move toward the cross. There is no value in mere suffering. But when suffering is a necessary part of forgetting ourselves and living for others, then it already partakes of the glorious resurrection.

Love is always a call to suffer, for it means to say "yes" to another. Tied to this readiness to give Eucharist to another is a "no" to any conflicting selfishness. That is why the liturgical Eucharist and our daily eucharistic service to others are equally a *sacrament* of self-giving and Jesus-giving, but also a *sacrifice* of ourselves as Jesus gives Himself totally to us.

A LIVING EUCHARIST

How the divinity and the humanity in Jesus Christ come together to form one divine-human Person can never be adequately explained by theologians. Nor will the unbelieving world come to hunger for the Eucharist by our arguments about transubstantiation and other fanciful theories to explain how Jesus Christ is found in bread and wine. Such mysteries are beyond the intellect of man to fathom.

Yet this does not mean that men and women cannot experience the total Person of Jesus Christ, energizing them into a new creation (2 Co 5:17). It means that Jesus becomes for us Eucharist as the Bread of Life when we bring that experience of God's energizing love, centered in the Eucharist, to each person we meet. The fullness of the Eucharist embraces the Body of Christ with all His members. Through the Eucharist we breathe a living prayer of reconciliation over the entire material universe to bring it also into the Body of Christ.

These beautiful words written by Teilhard de Chardin summarize very well the essence of this chapter:

Grant, O God, that when I draw near to the altar to communicate, I may henceforth discern the infinite perspectives hidden beneath the smallness and the nearness of the Host in which You are concealed. I have already accustomed myself to seeing beneath the stillness of that piece of bread, a devouring power which, in the words of the greatest Doctors of Your Church, far from being consumed by me, consumes me. Give me the strength to rise above the remaining illusions which tend to make me think of Your touch as circumscribed and momentary. I am beginning to understand: under the sacramental Species it is primarily through the 'accidents' of matter that You touch me, but, as a consequence, it is also through the whole universe in proportion as this ebbs and flows over me under Your primary influence. In a true sense the arms and the heart which You open to me are nothing less than all the united powers of the world which, penetrated and permeated to their depths by Your will, Your tastes and Your temperament, converge upon my being to form it, nourish it and bear it along towards the center of Your fire. In the Host it is my life that You are offering me, O Jesus.[11]

VII

Come Aside And Rest Awhile

For Christians who pour themselves out in apostolic giving to others, there seems to be a perennial tension between their work and their time for prayer. How much time must one give to prayer is a question constantly being asked by earnest Christians. What is usually presupposed is that somehow one must spend *some* time at least. This often can be an intellectual assent that may never become actualized in a daily time set aside to be "at leisure" with God. Or it may be appreciated and rewarded a quick half hour of spiritual reading or speeches said to God in vocal or discursive prayer over the liturgical readings of the day.

One of the greatest needs in our modern life is to have leisure time to touch God and spring into new meaningfulness. Our feverish activism makes it difficult for us to be quiet before the Holy of Holies. Psychically we enter into prayer with a frettish nervousness that pours over an exhausted body, through taut and tense nerves and muscles, to reach a psyche that knows no peace and joy.

COME TO SOME LONELY PLACE

Our mind conjures up, as apostles, new things we have yet to do for God. Instead of entering deeply into the sacred presence of God, we hang about the market places shopping for cheap bargains. For years we can pray in such anxious ways and yet our daily lives reflect little of change. Jesus continually calls us as He did His Disciples: "You must come away to some lonely place all by yourselves and rest for a while" (Mk 6:31). But are we completely convinced of the need to come apart and rest deeply in Him?

Even when we give formal time to prayer, do we not go to such prayer with a *doing* mentality? We want to receive something "practical" for our efforts. We want to pray so as to be effective apostles. We have been taught that we cannot be effective in the apostolate unless we pray. Time spent in prayer seemingly in an automatic way would bring fruitful blessings upon our daily activities.

Another criterion for prayer and the time when we give to it is often—"I pray at such and such a time, usually in the evening after work, because then I am relaxed and feel like praying." Many have no intimate contact with God at the beginning of their day because they go to pray seeking a good feeling or something they can receive from prayer. One can surely pray in the evening also, but I would like to stress in this chapter the absolute need for a deep centering upon God as the first act of our day.

Pragmatic reasons for prayer hardly bring about great results. I must see in prayer the supreme act of my life:—to adore, worship, love and desire to surrender my whole life to God, my loving Father. Otherwise my appreciation for prayer will be on the level of a man who sets aside mechanically a half hour each evening to spend with his wife and children, principally because he believes such time spent will make him a more effective man in business.

EXAMPLE OF JESUS

Jesus found night adoration and prayer to His Heavenly Father in the early hours of the morning to be a necessary part of the rhythm of His life. We read in St. Luke's Gospel:

> Now it was about this time that he went out into the hills to pray; and he spent the whole night in prayer to God (Lk 6:12).

Jesus usually prayed alone with His Heavenly Father, away from the activities of the day, even away from His Disciples. On their journeys they rise and seek Jesus who is already absorbed in early morning prayer before His Father. It is in such prayer that Jesus seeks the face of His Father. In His complete surrender of Himself to let the Father do with Him whatever He wishes, Jesus is bringing about the Kingdom of Heaven. The Spirit of God fills Him with filial trust before the goodness and holiness of His Father.

The example of Jesus praying to His Father during the dark night and in the early hours of the morning suggests to us that the rhythm Jesus found in His life should be a part also of our lives. He experienced the time of day to be up and about His Father's business. He knew the hard, monotonous work in the carpenter shop, weary muscles and a body that cried out for rest and sleep. He knew that, as the soft rays of the violet sun sunk in the west in Nazareth or on His apostolic journeys to preach the

Kingdom of God in Palestine, the evening was bringing to Him the rhythm of peace, rest, intimacy with His Father. He would sleep, but He would also adore His Father. Out of the darkness He would seek the flaming face of His Father, so full of creative love for His only begotten Son.

On the mountain tops of night, so calm, so still, all in darkness, His Father reached out to touch His Son and bring Him into new being. The fatigue of the day would dissolve in such energizing love of the Father. The darkness surrounding Jesus in nightly prayer would yield to the sunlight brilliance of the Father, coming to Him like fire, searing, burning, yet consuming Him not. Before such Brilliance Jesus surrendered.

> My food is to do the will of the one who sent me, and to complete his work (Jn 4:34).

Before such gentle love, Jesus could afford to become gentle and humble of heart. It was recreating Him according to that Mind so that the next day all who saw Him would see also the Heavenly Father.

Because Jesus could afford to be alone with the Father in darkness, He could also find Him with ease in the light of the day's activities. His Father sustained Him and all creatures in their being. In each event of every moment Jesus experienced the dynamic, active love of the Father working in Him and in all creatures around Him. "My Father goes on working and so do I" (Jn 5:17).

ONE WITH THE FATHER IN ACTION

Jesus freely consented to work at each moment during the day according to His Father's holy will only because

He had met the Father as His total sufficiency, His life-line (2 Co 3:5). Thus in all encounters with other human beings, Jesus could cast all care upon the Heavenly Father who cared for Him and all human beings (1 P 5:7). Jesus was able to meet the presence and loving activity of the Father in each person that He met because He had gone apart to be alone with His Father. He first found Him working deeply in His "heart," in the deepest reaches of his consciousness. It was there in the depths of His being, in His core or at His center, that He contemplated the Father as loving Him and constantly begetting Him into His image.

Deep down He felt the loving presence of the Father penetrating His whole being. No longer could He live independently of the Father but only in total consecration to do His holy will in all things.

> As you sent me into the world,
> I have sent them into the world,
> and for their sake I consecrate myself
> so that they too may be consecrated in truth (Jn 17:18).

Also into the darkness within Himself, where Jesus was tempted in all things save sin (Heb 4:15), did the Father penetrate with His loving light to bring His Son into total attachment to Himself. All throughout His hidden and public life, Jesus had to undergo, in deep prayer, the temptations, much as Eve, the feminine side of man in the Garden of Eden, to take the initiative to dispose of His life and talents as He would wish with no reference to the will of His Father. Yet in prayer Jesus learned not to yield to feed Himself by anything but by God's word. In prayer Jesus learned that power and glory in this world were to be rejected by humble worship to God alone. "You must worship the Lord your God, and serve him alone" (Lk 4:8).

In prayer that must have known moments of great aridity similar to that prayer Jesus uttered in the agony of Gethsemane, Jesus pushed Himself to new depths of holiness and loving surrender as He cried out "Father!" Regardless of how He feels in such nightly prayer, Jesus is present to His Father in loving surrender as Gift to Giver. Prayer is emptying to be filled by the Father. But Jesus can empty Himself completely only because He has deeply and intensely experienced, in praying in His heart, the extent of His Father's emptying of Himself as total Gift to His Son.

NIGHT VIGIL

Day and night alternate in a natural rhythm of life. The sun shines; everything is bathed in its light. During the day there is great movement, much variety, business, multiplicity. The sun sets and nature all around man takes on slowly a new rhythm. The day's activities yield to a global presence of peace and oneness between man and the world of growing darkness around him. Night is for rest, intimacy, sleep, restoring of one's powers. It is a time to enter into eternity to receive a call to ultimacy. At night in the intimacy of our homes and the love of our loved ones, we relax. New powers to love come forth in the trustful atmosphere of being at peace and at one with those we love.

Night is also a time to pray, to be alone with God. It is the favored time for all contemplatives to come alive with spiritual eyes that are gifted to penetrate through the opaqueness of the day's false lights to see the eternal light of God's abiding love shining through the sorrows and even the joys of the day. It is the time to be swept up into the timelessness of the eternal now where there is little of changing movements and variety. There is darkness that covers all things into a oneness that tells us we are all one great gift of God. "All night, Yahweh, I remember your name and observe your Law" (Ps 119:55).

> Though the nooses of the wicked tighten round me,
> I do not forget your Law.
> I get up at midnight to thank you
> for the righteousness of your rulings (Ps 119: 61-62).

The night was made for prayer, for returning to the Beginning and the End of our lives, to God, our All. It is a time to worship Him and to surrender. It is a time for loving Him without words but in a daily experience of fidelity because God has been so faithful to us. "Stretch out your hands towards the sanctuary, bless Yahweh night after night!" (Ps 134: 2).

It is good to pray to God at the close of the day. But it is even better to rise from our sleep after some hours of rest to praise God. There was a time in early Christianity when not merely monks but also lay persons, including children, rose from sleep to praise God. In our objectivization and putting things neatly into boxes, we have allowed monks and professional contemplatives who pursue God day and night to continue this practice. But few of us who engage in active work within the context of the bustle of the market place ever think that this practice might also become a vital part of our lives, that it might just be an important element in our apostolate that will allow us to be pure channels of God's grace to those we are privileged to serve.

Have we at least had the courage to examine our prayer-life to see whether God has not been calling us into deeper prayer, of a contemplative nature? Again, avoiding any pragmatic reasoning that we should put this practice into our lives because it will help our apostolate, let us ask ourselves rather whether God has not been insistently knocking at the door of our hearts (Rv 3:20) to come aside in the darkness of deep night to pray and adore Him in the wasteful leisure of *doing* nothing except merely *being* towards Him?

St. John Chrysostom exhorted his 4th century Christians to rise from their sleep to pray at night: "Why does the Psalmist speak of praying in the night? He teaches us that the night is not to be completely spent in sleep and he shows that at night the prayers are purer, when also the mind is more uplifted and we are more at ease."[1] If God has led us to a more simplified prayer where, in the night of deeper faith and self-surrender, we have passed the oasis of images and words and even sweet feelings and affections, His Spirit then pushes us to pray at a time when we are more "at ease." It is no longer a question of whether we can pray better at night than during the day. It becomes an urgency, the same urgency that "forces" lovers to find places, especially at night, to be alone with each other for longer time than "clock-time" of daylight permits.

I see more and more that one should not seek reasons to convince people of the value of such night vigils. Such prayer can only be experienced and when one comes into the experience of waiting in the early hours of the morning, that has not yet seen the diffusiveness of daylight, for the coming of the Lord Jesus and it happens in an experience beyond words and images and feelings, then such prayer-time becomes a part, a *necessary* part of one's daily rhythm. I have written about this waiting for the Parousia to happen in *Inward Stillness:*

Praying at night after one has enjoyed several hours of
deep, refreshing sleep, offers the Christian an experience
of the Parousia as already here. Night is usually a time of
indeterminateness; blackness ill-defines reality around us.
We are thrown back into a primal fear of death and the
unknown. Praying at night dispels such darkness and
fear.[2]

The peak of the Christian experience of always
waiting for Christ to come and heal us is reached in such
quiet prayer for He comes in our very crying out. The bride
cries out for the Bridegroom to come. There is longing, a
thirst that nothing on this earth can quench. Love burns
and ignites in the absence of the Beloved. Like the Bride in
the Song of Songs, such a contemplative cries out in the
early hours of the still dark morning:

On my bed, at night, I sought him
whom my heart loves.
I sought but did not find him . . .
I will seek him whom my heart loves.
. . . I sought but did not find him.
The watchmen came upon me
on their rounds in the City:
'Have you seen him whom my heart loves?' (Sg 3:1-3).

The night resembles the darkness within your soul.
Groping with no sureness coming from your own power,
you cry out for the Light of the world to come and dispel
the darkness within you. In the quiet of the night you know
the areas of your inner self that need healing, that are not
yet redeemed by the love of Jesus. You have an inner clarity of your darkness. You let go of your proud self-reliance.
Faith deepens as there is no other support to prevent you

from sinking deeper into the ocean of darkness that surrounds you. "Lord, Jesus Christ, Son of God, have mercy on me, a sinner!" The Jesus Prayer or merely the sacred name of Jesus becomes your constant fixation as you stretch yourself to meet His healing presence.

And He does come! Softly as the first rays of light, the Risen Jesus covers you with His healing power. His light covers you and dispels all darkness from your being. The great paradox of Christianity is experienced: in death to self there is resurrection to a new life in Christ. He was absent but now He is present. St. Paul grasped the paradox of night with Christ which is transformed into brilliant day:

> No, you are all sons of light and sons of the day; we do not belong to the night or to darkness, so we should not go on sleeping as everyone else does, but stay wide awake and sober. Night is the time for sleepers to sleep and drunkards to be drunk, but we belong to the day and we should be sober (1 Th 5: 5-8).

A RECONCILER OF THE WORLD TO CHRIST

As one renders oneself more completely docile to the workings of the Holy Spirit in contemplative prayer, the Spirit leads such a contemplative into a vivid experience of being one with the whole world. Here too he experiences this oneness on two tensioned levels. The first is the oneness with a broken, sinful, fragmented world that knows not the redemption of Jesus Christ. The darkness that surrounds the contemplative who rises to enter into a vigil of waiting for the coming of the Lord into his world again is a vivid reminder of the spiritual darkness that covers the world living outside of the light of Christ. St. Paul describes this "oneness" with a crippled world:

> The whole creation is eagerly waiting for God to reveal his sons. It was not for any fault on the part of creation that it was made unable to attain its purpose, it was made so by God; but creation still retains the hope of being freed, like us, from its slavery to decadence, to enjoy the same freedom and glory as the children of God. From the beginning till now the entire creation, as we know, has been groaning in one great act of giving birth; and not only creation, but all of us who possess the first fruits of the Spirit, we too groan inwardly as we wait for our bodies to be set free. For we must be content to hope that we shall be saved—our salvation is not in sight, we should not have to be hoping for it if it were—but, as I say, we must hope to be saved since we are not saved yet—it is something we must wait for with patience (Rm 8: 18-25).

Although the contemplative knows in his heart that Jesus is truly risen and has wedded Himself forever to remain inside the Father's creation as a leaven in a mass of dough, yet he knows also, impelled by the same Holy Spirit that drove Jesus into the dark desert, that Jesus in His Body, the Church, in the members in whom He lives, becomes risen in that place where the Christian in believing faith calls His presence into being. Think of the great responsibility of being a Christian, to have been given a faith that assures us that if we persecute the members of the Body of Christ in any way, we persecute Jesus Christ, as St. Paul learned from Christ Himself on the road to Damascus! But more importantly, think of the responsibility under the inspiration of the Holy Spirit to believe that the living members are capable of calling Jesus, the Healer, into specific areas of this world that is groaning in travail!

Jesus not only will not come in the full *Parousia* if such Christians do not wait expectantly for His coming but He will not be coming *this* night and the next day into this world in which such Christians live if they do not "direct" His presence. God is free to come and go as He wishes. But in the economy of salvation in which God has so loved this world as to give it His only begotten Son (Jn 3:16), He brings us life through Jesus in His Church, in His preached Word, in His sacramental encounters with people of the world. The peak of God's self-giving is enacted in the Holy Eucharist, the climax of all other sacramental presences of Jesus Christ. Yet contemplative prayer is the continued state of remaining in that eucharistic presence of Jesus giving Himself to the Father on behalf of the suffering world. Such prayer of faith is fortified in the Eucharist by the individual Christian contemplatives as they receive daily that Bread of Life.

In such night vigils, distances shrink into nothingness. Everything is reduced to darkness and light, death and life, the absence and the presence of Jesus Christ. As the Christian cries out for the coming of the Lord into his own darkness, he opens up to the darkness revealed to him in the previous day: darkness in war-torn areas, in the suffering patients in innumerable hospital beds throughout the world, in the prison cells behind walls. There is darkness in the hearts of politicians who play one country against another in selling arms so that they may gain profits and yet in a few years millions will die from such selfish exploitation. What darkness will never be removed from the hearts of the depressed, the psychotics who live in cells that suffocate human growth and know no love, no exit! The daily newspapers give the targets and the heart enflamed with love for God gives the direction for the healing of Jesus to come again into that place and heal all the sicknesses and diseases of the people of God (Mt 4: 23-24; 9:35). Through such contemplatives crying out for the Parousia, the Presence of the healing Lord Jesus, He does come in a marvelous way known only to those of such great faith and those who witness the effects of the healing Lord in their lives.

> And when he saw the crowds, he felt sorry for them because they were harassed and dejected, like sheep without a shepherd (Mt 9: 36).

ONENESS WITH SINNERS

St. Therese of Lisieux made the resolution to want always, even in the life to come, to remain seated "at the table of sinners" in her solidarity with them. She wanted to share their food, somewhat like the prodigal son who ended up by coveting the food of beasts. For them she offered the mediocrity of her prayer and the obscurity and difficulties of her faith, believing that, in spite of her own poverty before the Lord, God's goodness brought graces to the needy. St. Dominic also was obsessed by the thought of sinners: "What will become of sinners?" he constantly asked God in prayer.

> God had granted him a special grace of prayer for sinners, the poor, the afflicted; he bore their misery in the innermost sanctuary of his compassion, and the tears which he shed were a clear manifestation of the ardor of the sentiment which burned within him.[3]

If such communion with God makes it possible that the contemplative in deep prayer is obsessed by the darkness existing in the hearts of those who live without knowing their Heavenly Father, it is because theologically such apostolic love, the fruit of the Holy Spirit in true authentic Christian prayer, is grounded on the nature of God. In the Old Testament we see this concept clearly brought out in the meaning of God who is Yahweh, God among His people.[4] God is a faithful presence of love to His suffering people. He is concerned with His people. He is the healing Yahweh who wants to bring life to His Chosen (Ex 15:26).

And those contemplatives, who in deep prayer have entered into eternity beyond time, into the *kairos* or the eternal *now* time of God's healing love, can have no other desire than that of God to be a loving presence among the broken ones of this earth. And thus the gentle, compassionate Jesus continues to walk about our cities at night to stretch out His forgiving hand to the prostitute, a healing glance to one suffering physical or mental anguish. But He is alive because contemplatives are alive in faith to His eternal, loving presence within them and through them toward the whole suffering world.

Apostolic work begins in deep contemplative prayer as the Spirit moves such men and women of ardent faith to spend themselves to be all things, as St. Paul wished, to win all men for Christ. Prayer then is not an activity done in order to protect the apostle from the contagions of the world which he must touch if he is to bring it to Christ. He goes to prayer to become an apostle, an experienced witness to the resurrection of Jesus Christ. It is in prayer that the Holy Spirit makes him, as Jesus promised (Jn 15: 26-27) a witness to Jesus Lord.

MORNING PRAYER

Many readers will find difficulty because of their "home" situation or their fluid schedule that often does not allow a disciplined program to be set up so that they can be assured some solid hours of sleep, say about three, and some few hours of sleep after they have prayed their night vigil. God can never be outdone in generosity. He never gives Himself in only one way to all people serious about prayer. As they advance in contemplative prayer of deeper faith and less of their own activity, such Christians will seek those precious moments of prayer at night whenever such is possible in keeping with their state of life and their fulfillment of their God-given responsibilities.

But for all who are desirous of advancing in deeper prayer, some extended time in the early morning, after they have awakened from their sleep to begin a new day, becomes a necessity. They will find that the vocal prayers of the Office recited by themselves or in common with others or those prayers of the morning Liturgy are not sufficient to bring them into the *centering* necessary to keep them in a state of attention to God's presence during the rest of the busy day. It has always seemed to me quite evident that this is of obligation on all Christians but especially for those who are advancing in a contemplative form of prayer. There can be little progress in deep faith, hope and love if one does not carve out the first moments of consciousness as the first fruits of the day and consecrate them to God in deep silence and adoration.

Our sleep is like a mini-death. We wake up in our consciousness to a new day. We put aside what went before in the newness of the life that awaits us. There is need to live out the symbol of our Baptism. We must enter again into the indeterminateness of our interior selves and there call the Risen Lord to become, by the power of the Spirit praying within us, indeed our Lord and Savior (1 Co 12:3). We need this first, "prime time" in which to present ourselves before the Lord and make our loving surrender to allow Him to be Master of our lives this day. One author writes about the necessity to give the first moments of awakening to the Lord in prayer:

> A necessary, indispensible exercise, for everything begins from there, from this light, from this strength. The liturgical activity itself only takes on its complete validity when it is enlightened by this watchful faith, which discerns its sacred meaning and consents inwardly to what it expresss outwardly. This is why the exercise of prayer normally precedes everything else.[5]

Such a person of prayer turns himself at the very beginning of his active day to be grounded in the light of Christ and His values as found in Holy Scripture. Thus St. Paul likens our rising from sleep to a rising from the dead into a new life with Christ who enlightens us with His light:

> . . . but anything exposed by the light will be illuminated and anything illuminated turns into light. That is why it is said:
> Wake up from your sleep,
> rise from the dead,
> and Christ will shine on you (Ep 5: 14).

The success of our day will depend on our *centering* deeply in the early moments of the day before we become too "distracted" by the multiple activities that fill our busy lives. If we put such *centering* off until the afternoon or

evening, we can see that we will meet the daily events only
with our own power. We will judge according to St. Paul's
"carnal mind." The Spirit will not fill us with the sifting
knowledge that makes the Word of God a living Word,
like a two-edged sword that "can slip through the place
where the soul is divided from the spirit . . . it can judge
the secret emotions and thoughts . . . everything is un-
covered and open to the eyes of the one to whom we must
give account of ourselves" (Heb 4: 12-13).

We touch the basic truth in our relationships with
God. He is God, our total strength. Unless He builds, we
labor in vain. We can perform many heroic acts in an attempt to educate people, give away even millions, as St.
Paul says, even give our bodies to be burned, yet if we do
not speak with the love of God in us, we are simply "a
gong booming or a cymbal clashing" (1 Co 13:2). It is imperative, therefore, that we go to the well of living water in
early morning to drink unto life. "The water that I shall
give will turn into a spring inside him, welling up to eternal
life" (Jn 4:14).

This is to be baptized each day unto a new life, not
through water alone but by the Spirit that Jesus releases
within our hearts (Jn 3:5). And yet how few Christians are
ready to give God daily the first hour of consciousness in
which they can humbly beg His mercy and love and surrender themselves in loving service to Him? Is there any
true Christian apostolate without aligning ourselves to the
Life-Giver, Jesus Christ? It must be the power of Jesus
within us that allows us to bring forth fruit with Him. He
clearly preached this to all of His followers:

I am the vine,
you are the branches.

Whoever remains in me, with me in him,
bears fruit in plenty;
for cut off from me you can do nothing.
Anyone who does not remain in me
is like a branch that has been thrown away
—he withers;
. . . If you remain in me
and my words remain in you,
    you may ask what you will
    and you shall get it (Jn 15: 5-7).

WASTING TIME

For busy people in a hurry to bring the whole world to Christ, spending an hour in silent adoration, without words, images, even with little affection, above all, with little concrete criterion that anything is happening, even that they are really praying, seems a waste of time. It is true, as one moves into the prayer of faith, the beginning stage of contemplation, the definite criteria, open to our own rational judgment, vanish into "obscurity." This is perhaps the main reason why there are so few contemplatives in our Western world that is so geared to the scientific and the discursively controlled knowledge.

St. John of the Cross describes this letting go of such "known" knowledge to enter into a nakedness of faith:

We can apply, then, what Christ says about the narrow gate to the sensitive portion of man, and what He says about the straight way to the spiritual or rational part of his soul. Since He proclaims that few find it, we ought to note the cause: Few there are with the knowledge and desire for entering upon this supreme nakedness and emptiness of spirit. As this path on the high mount of perfection is narrow and steep, it demands travelers who are not weighed down by the lower part of their nature, nor burdened in the higher part. This is a venture in which God alone is sought and gained, thus only God ought to be sought and gained.[6]

And yet such a prayer of faith is not wasting time but is the most positive gaining of an entrance into God's real time. It is a new way of seeing, as has been already mentioned in preceding chapters that touched upon the apophatic, positive elements in the doctrine on contemplative prayer of the Greek Fathers. From unknowing through our own intellectual powers, we move into the gifted knowledge of God who reveals to us in an intuitive grasp what cannot be attained in any mere human way. It is what St. Paul speaks of about our hidden selves growing so that Christ may live in our hearts through faith, so that then we will, with all the saints, have the strength to grasp the breadth and the length, the height and the depth in knowing the love of Christ which is "beyond all knowledge" and thus we become filled with the "utter fulness of God" (Ep 3: 16-19).

Leonard Boase gives a very positive description of such a contemplative prayer of faith:

> It is a communion with God in which the soul is aware of His reality and of His presence by a sort of 'six-sense' or 'second-sight' or 'telepathy' which is specifically different from the kind of certainty that He exists attained by logical demonstration. It is a certainty different also from the assent of faith given by Christians in every day conditions; but it differs from this not specifically, but only because that same certainty of faith has moved, so to speak, into the sensitive focus of consciousness.[7]

REST UNTO FULL ACTIVITY

Early morning alone with God can never be an end in itself. It is always the stirring of one who was asleep unto full life. *Centering* upon God has meaning insofar as God impels us through His Spirit of love to move outwardly into the world to "unveil" His sacred presence already there. Both in such faithful prayer and in one's activities throughout the busy day, the contemplative, like a prophet, is the messenger and as mediator with Jesus Christ, the fulfillment of all prophets, and is centered upon God's world. He is filled with God's very own compassionate love for His children. He, the prophet and mediator with Jesus Christ, becomes one with his people. Yet by deep faith he is also one with the indwelling God whom he adores in prayerful worship.

With Moses he stands before the face of God and prays boldly that if God does not forgive the sins of His people, then he prays: " . . . blot me out from the book that you have written" (Ex 32: 32). With St. Paul whose words are beautifully commented on by St. Symeon the New Theologian (+ 1022), the modern prophet "would not even wish to enter into the Kingdom of Heaven if he had to be separated from them."[8]

Having rested in the love of God that continually on deeper levels of consciousness begets the contemplative into new identity as a child loved infinitely by God the Father in Christ Jesus, such a person of prayer is filled with love for his brothers and sisters throughout the whole world. He has entered into a new global oneness with humanity, with individuals in all of their uniqueness as loved individually by God. The test of true prayer, especially if it flows from an outpouring of the Holy Spirit through deeper infusion of faith, hope and love, must always be one's life style that will be the fruit to judge the authenticity of such prayer of faith.

Rooted in God in the early hours of the morning, we can go forth into the chaotic world of so much apparent meaninglessness, sin, darkness, frustration and, with hope ringing in our hearts, we can serve our brothers and sisters as divine providence brings them into our lives. The degree that we have been grounded in that intimate union with Jesus Christ and His Heavenly Father through their Spirit of love in the morning, to that same degree will we be able to surrender at each moment our whole life to be put under His loving power. Every thought, word and deed become surrendered totally to Him.

And yet, in a marvelous intuitive grasp, such a contemplative knows by God's knowledge poured into his heart that God is everywhere, in all persons, in all events. Such an apostle is ready to give God true freedom to act in his life and in the lives of others as He would wish for His greater glory. He finds God's "Shekinah" or glory as God's loving presence transforming each event into a transcendence of loving union of all things into the Allness of God. This glory he perceives not as a static thing. Such a prophet in the modern world moves through this world in union with Jesus Christ, in a similar manner as He did in Palestine during His earthly life. He does not tell the world so much that we must give glory to God. He points out to all whom he meets that God is a glory, a loving energy found in each event. By lovingly surrendering to this presence of god, such an apostle becomes a presence of God's uncreated energies of love pouring around and permeating from within each person that he encounters.

Centered prayer in early morning means centered

prayer throughout the day in each moment of "worldly" activity. The contemplative thus grows in such activities to find God everywhere. The material world is no longer an obstacle but the "place" where the contemplative unveils the inner presence of God and brings it all to a conscious level of adoration and loving service. The words of Gerard Manley Hopkins form a fitting close to this chapter on contemplative prayer as apostolic prayer:

> I say more: the just man justices;
> Keeps grace: that keeps all his goings graces;
> Acts in God's eye what in God's eye he is—
> Christ—for Christ plays in ten thousand places,
> Lovely in limbs, and lovely in eyes not his
> To the Father through the features of men's faces.[9]

8

In His Presence

In that delightful modern odyssey into the inner world of expanded consciousness of Carlos Casteneda, *Journey to Ixtlan,* Don Juan teaches his disciple the necessity of "stopping the world." The disciple went into the desert and in silence listened to the real world for the first time. He saw what was always there, but most people fail to see. Don Juan explains:

> What stopped inside you yesterday was what people have been telling you the world is like. You see, people tell us from the time that we are born that the world is such and such and so and so, and naturally we have no choice but to see the world the way people have been telling us it is.[1]

Technology has cast the human race into a trance. We walk about sleeping, unaware of an inner world of power, beauty, joyful play and infinite love. Science has built a complete religion, based on the paradise myth of a material world of flowing oil and money, pontificated by the moguls of industry, attained by hard work on the part of all who wish to share in the kingdom of this earth. But we are being shocked out of our new religious torpor by the impending cataclysmic signs flashing ominously in the West.

We see the need to turn "within" in order to make contact with a sacred presence that is more powerful than we are. A sacred meaningfulness that gives ultimate direction beyond man's immediate selfish needs. Modern man eagerly cries out to contact the *numinous* world, described by Rudolf Otto.[2] This cannot be taught. It can only be evoked, awakened in the mind by the transcendent power of God's Spirit.

It is inwardly that we must go, into our *hearts*, that scriptural symbol of the interior *locus* or "place" where man meets his Maker and Beloved in ever-expanding consciousness. This consciousness of the divine presence, as loving, uncreating energies, abiding within us and without us, in each material atom of the universe, grows as we tune in more consistently to listen to God's revealing Word as He speaks to us in the cosmic signs of the material universe. His Word also speaks to us and reveals God's *numinous* presence in the signs of written Scripture as well as recorded history of the past and of the present moments in history now being lived and created with man's cooperation. We can read these signs also inside of us in the depths of our own consciousness and unconscious.

THE JOURNEY WITHIN

God has made man to live "naturally" at home with Him. God's *numinous* or sacred presence was meant to be discovered within man's inner depths of his being as well as inside the material layers of the world around him. Man has always sought to look upon the face of God through myths and legends, symbols and sacred rituals. It is our technical world with its own religion of matter that has extinguished in man's world the light whereby he can *see* God everywhere, live always in His loving presence, be joyful like a happy child, be creative in developing the potentials that lie dormant unto so much love activity in man's universe.

Carl Jung lamented the fact that Western man had become impoverished in his use of myths and symbols to transcend his horizontal optic in order to make contact with the Ultimate Ground of his being. The technological power placed in man's hands makes it difficult for him to experience a "creature-consciousness" before the awesome "Otherness" of God as totally transcendent and holy. Because we have lost the *Otherness* of God as the Ultimate Source of all being, we have also lost the presence of God within us, more intimately to ourselves than we ourselves are, to use St. Augustine's oft-quoted statement.

There is a renewed interest in the *sacred,* not as a quality attached any more to places or persons or rites, but as an ambience, a milieu, into which we enter by an expansion of consciousness to touch God deeply and to be touched by Him.

Carl Jung described the importance of the human psyche in the development of the world.

> The psyche is the world's pivot: not only is it the one great condition for the existence of a world at all, it is also an intervention in the existing natural order, and no one can say with certainty where this intervention will finally end.[3]

It is *inside,* into his *heart,* that man must go. It is a terrifying journey that few of us have the courage to make. Many of us are attracted to the possibility of living constantly in loving communication and we make a valiant beginning. Most of us come running to *surface* after a short time. We miss the noise, multiplicity, the gaudy lights of the carnival and the raucous pitch of the hawker enticing us to see his side-show, "the greatest wonder on earth." The cotton candy and the sticky carnival apples delight us and make us forget what could have been.

We possess the power for undoing ourselves and putting off the whole process of becoming healed and wholly integrated persons, the ones that correspond to the name and person God knows us to be when from the depths of our being He calls us by our name (Is 43:1). We are masters at avoiding a confrontation with the real person that we are. We can play games, put up masks, become distracted by the words and values that people around us live by. We can even busy ourselves "saying" prayers or, even in so-called "silent" prayer, refuse in real silence to look at our inner feelings, look at both the light and the darkness that are struggling for possession of us. As long as we indulge in such game-playing, it means we are afraid to be silent. We fear to look inwardly and honestly ask for healing from the Transcendent God when we see through genuine self-knowledge what needs to be sacrificed, what needs to be transformed.

QUICK PANACEAS

Most persons, eager to enter into a state of continuous communication with God, seek relatively quick ways, techniques, by which they can gain the Kingdom of Heaven. The Gospel speaks of seeds that are sown into the earth and grow slowly, day and night, almost imperceptibly. With this age's penchant for gimmicks and institutes, surely, we think, there must be some school, book or teacher that on a quick weekend can reveal to us the mysteries of praying always and turn us into instant "mystics" without much money or effort spent in the process.

Nothing could be more erroneous and against the Gospel teaching. Although God is truly present everywhere as both the Old and New Testaments teach, and we really do move and have all our being in Him (Ac 17:28), still to grasp this reality and to live according to this as a permanent state of transcendent consciousness comes about only through long years of hard work on our part to purify our interior eyes. Through God's continuous loving presence in each new experience, He draws us into new levels of awareness of His sacred presence to us in life's situations.

Prayer admits of many levels of expansion of our consciousness into an ever deepening awareness that God and we form a unity in love. Christian prayer through the faith, hope and love infused into the one praying by the Spirit of Jesus Christ is an on-going process of discovering not only the abyss that separates the Absolute, all-Holy God from us sinners but also discovering the depths of oneness that exists between us and God in the very depths of our being. Growth in prayer is, therefore, a growth in awareness of God, especially as He lives and acts through His infinite love within us.

Awareness of God's presence leads us into His self-giving communication through His Word and His Holy Spirit. We actually become more and more aware of God's communication of Himself as Gift of Himself in perfect love, personalized, stretching in human terms unto death, the death of the Cross in Jesus Christ for each of us human beings. St. Paul experienced in the communication through prayer that God really died for *him* (Ga 2:20).

Communication of God in His loving self-giving to us calls out a response in our return communication with God. This response is not merely during our formal, solitary prayer time, but such a response, to be a true, growing experience, pushes our consciousness of our new identity with God to new heights. We, in prayer, experience our new identity as children of so loving a Heavenly Father, whose love is constantly being imaged by Jesus Christ, His only begotten Son through His Holy Spirit. We push ourselves to deeper levels of consciousness of the indwelling Trinity, firstly within us. This is within the context of thought and realization. The Father and the Son truly come and dwell within us with their Spirit (Jn 14:23). This impels us outwardly into the larger context of our life. Struggle is the word for pushing ourselves to cross from here to there, always striving to attain to new levels beyond the present limitation.

Grace or the uncreated energies of God are always operating within our lives. Yet for most of us how difficult it is to yield to God's loving, transforming power! Piet Fransen, S.J. writes:

> We, men, are not easily persuaded to give up ourselves; we behave like the drowning man, who dazed and paralyzed by fear, does not dare to jump off the sinking ship . . . the surrender grace wants to lead us to is nothing short of a total surrender to God, sealed with the absoluteness of Christ Himself; for it is that which He seeks to effect in us through His Spirit . . . Riddance of self, or better, decentralization from self to God alone, causes such a sundering right down to the lower psychic regions that the mystics

have found no better expression suited to describe their experience than an extremely bitter death, a "dark night" for both the senses and the spirit . . . To most of the faithful, this deep spiritual agony occurs, perhaps, around the time of the death of the body, or otherwise in purgatory.[4]

DISINTEGRATION

Part of our unwillingness to let go and allow God to be sole Master within our lives comes from the state of disintegration in which we find ourselves. Through the contagion of collective sins, the result of the original fall in mankind, man now finds himself disintegrated, not living according to his nature as God wants Him to do and has destined him with the potential to attain. The body now is a burden, something that brings us tiredness, suffering and pain. It is all too often an instrument of evil desires. The triple hierarchic harmony of body, soul and spirit has been broken. Endowed with freedom, we can so readily choose evil, unmindful of our true nature to be loving children of God who loves us infinitely. *Dypsychia* or double-souled is the term the early Christians gave to this state of disintegration. St. Paul well describes it from his own personal observation:

> In my inmost self I dearly love God's Law, but I can see that my body follows a different law that battles against the law which my reason dictates. This is what makes me a prisoner of that law of sin which lives inside my body (Rm 7: 22-23).

RE-INTEGRATION

In such a fallen state only a true and genuine re-integration of body-soul-spirit relationships will allow us to enter into our true, natural state of being consciously one in communication with the Ultimate Reality, God, in whose image and likeness we have been created. God created man to grow into an integrated human being through vital relationships.

Such an integration process must go hand in hand from one level of relationships to the other. The dichotomy that pits matter against spirit, body and soul, must be set aside as one grows into a harmonious integration and a wholeness of body, soul and spirit relationships. Here the yogic techniques and other Eastern Christian methods can be of great help in disciplining the body and mind to make the whole man attentive to the movements of God's Spirit. In our affluent, self-indulging society, the various physical postures of Hatha Yoga can help Western man pull himself together in body, mind and spirit before he begins to travel inwardly to deeper levels of union with the Absolute.

Many Christians have inherited a prejudice. When they hear the word *yoga*, they unfortunately condemn something they really do not understand. I speak here only of those bodily and mental exercises that are based on the isometric principle of inducing tension and then relaxation in order to experience an integrating force that allows one gradually to eliminate the concentration-dispersing thoughts and mental pre-occupations that prevent one from moving inwardly toward the point of perfect mental stillness.[5] Such yogic postures together with breath control and other purification exercises can recondition the body by giving it suppleness and vitality. These exercises are to flow easily over into an inner control that removes any immoderation in the use of emotions, intellect and will. Here the whole world of the Eastern Christians called *praxis* or the ascetical life, of control of the thoughts, of the bodily and emotional appetites, is a necessary part of our continued growth into deeper levels of consciousness of God's abiding presence within us. Fasting, vigils, continence, corporal and spiritual works of mercy find their way into our lives as we live in a simplification of all of our appetites to the domination of the indwelling Trinity, leading us to the moderation proper to each of us individually.

CRITICAL AWARENESS

The more we remain in this harmony of body, soul and spirit, the more we will be capable of receiving God's communication of Himself in love which is indeed always going on but we are woefully unaware of it. We will be in touch with the "really real" and understand that at the center of our deepest awareness, beyond our habitual preconditioning of sense and emotional and intellectual responses, we are gradually purified of our false ego-orientation in order to open ourselves toward the Allness of God.

God brings us gradually into a critical awareness that the Greek Fathers called *nepsis*. This means a "sober vigilance," an inner attentiveness to God's presence and a "passionate indifference," to quote Teilhard de Chardin's phrase to seek always only what is pleasing to God. It is a mental balance, an internal, disposition of attention to the movement of God's Spirit, leading us to true discernment of how we should react to any given situation or temptation according to our true dignity as God's loving children. In this state we are not moved impulsively by our own passions, but we hold ourselves in abeyance until we know what this or that thought is all about in reference to God's

Logos. God becomes the sole, living criterion of our choices. Freedom becomes ultimately our choosing always the good according to God's *Logos.* This is true integration of ourselves according to the likeness of God, brought about by fidelity to the interior living Word of God within us.

Only by means of a continuous single-minded effort can this process in the long run become a constant *habitus,* bringing about transformation by excluding all obstacles that stand in the way of such inter-penetration of God and man in expanded consciousness that we could call "prayer of the heart." K.G. von Durchheim describes the development of the sense of critical self-awareness:

> It is the awakening of, the separating out and, as it were, the making articulate a new sense that can smell out inner truth. Such work requires the development of a sensitivity which will enable us reliably to perceive all deviations from the true inner order. In particular we need to become susceptible to that within us which knows beyond any doubt whether we are wrongly or rightly centered. In this way critical awareness, being the means by which we progress, becomes active in each aim and aspect of a man's life.[6]

Such an inner discipline does not come easily or quickly. It is a state of physical, psychical and spiritual silencing of all desires outwardly toward any object to possess it in self-love. It is a state of inner tranquillity or disinterestedness which is far removed from the bane of true contemplation and presence to God, namely, quietism, that means having no interest in anything. The disciplined detachment taught by all spiritual directors in regard to higher contemplation is the removal of all self-centeredness in our desires and the placing of all our desires under the dominating desire of God's directing will. This allows us then to desire the things of this world in the best possible way, according to God's measure and not our own egoistic manner of exploitation out of self-love.

EXPANSION IN PRAYER AND INNER SILENCE

In order to foster the proper attitude of seeking to see God in all things, we must learn to withdraw from the material world and things in order to find God at the heart of matter. To enter into the inner reality of things we must learn to leave the periphery, the noise, competition, all-absorbing anxieties and fears that militate against the silence and calm necessary for us to listen to God communicate Himself to us. We have already spoken of the physical silence of our bodily members as well as the various psychic silencing of our emotions, imagination, memory, intellect and will. But the most profound and necessary silence that allows us to live always in the presence of God and to surrender to His communication of Himself to us in prompt obedience to His holy will is the harmony between our spirit and God's Spirit. It is here that heart speaks to heart in the language of self-surrendering love. This is a state of highest expanded consciousness brought about by an increased infusion of faith, hope and love by the Holy Spirit. It is only the Holy Spirit who can assure us that we are united with God and truly growing in greater loving union. It is also the Holy Spirit who brings forth His gifts and fruit in our relationships toward others. Our lives, now rooted more deeply in the ultimate, reflect more exactly than at any other earlier state the worth of our prayer-life. We live as we pray; we pray as we live.

It is absolutely necessary for all of us to preserve by God's grace and our constant cooperation that inner silence and solitude within our "hearts." We cannot all be called to an external desert and solitude, but we must find easily during our busy days that internal "space" within us that is created by a desire or hunger and thirst that will never be satisfied with any created being. It is in this deep loneliness of the solitude that deepest activities will begin. Thomas Merton writes:

> It is here that you discover, act without motion, labor that is profound repose, vision in obscurity and beyond all desire, a fulfillment whose limits extend to infinity.[7]

In man's heart he learns to descend and there listen to the transcendent God who is lovingly present with His uncreated energies that seek to transform man into his full nature as a loving child of God. Such effective prayer and contemplative, silent listening will awaken a deeper sense of consciousness of the divine intelligence, bring into our experience a greater good and inner meaning and relationship of all things in us and around us in their ultimate ground of being, in God Himself. The prayer of the heart becomes an experience of deep presence of God and a mystery of communication through our gradual transformation into Truth, into the growth of freedom in the Spirit.

Daily we open our consciousness to the Divine energies, as we expect greater wisdom and guidance. Listening to the inner voice of God's communicating presence, we will learn how to respond in harmony with

God's leadings. In awe, wonder and joyfulness before the Creator and Indwelling Father, I can listen to Him as He reveals through His Son and Spirit His secrets, His delicate promptings toward new levels of transformation into a new creation (2 Co 5:17). Such a prayer of the heart, with its constant fidelity in life's events of each day to God's holy will, the endurance of the inner desert, wilderness, suffering and purification, that are found there, brings us into a state of movement and tension. There is the tension of being in God with peace and tranquillity and that of not-being in Him with its accompanying darkness and demonic forces that rise up from our past to haunt us into crippling fears and inner anxieties.

God reveals Himself in the darkness of our own intellectual powers. Throughout the day we find now very little joy in remembering His presence. He seems so far from us as we grow in living in His presence. We seem so unworthy of His loving presence, so sinful in our selfish loves. We truly enter into the "cloud of unknowing" and we relinquish our control over ourselves and over God and the world we have been creating according to our new needs. This is that state of unconsciousness within us in which the untapped regions beneath the surface of existence are revealed. When we reach this state that is devoid of all human thought and ideas, we are given by God's grace and mercy a kind of knowledge of God that our ordinary consciousness and efforts could not provide. Part of this stage of the "cloud of unknowing" is characterized by inner healing of memories.

INNER HEALING

We are never persons who begin to meet God for the first time today in this moment. We meet God through the prisms of our many "yesterdays" which have all had an influence upon our today relationships with God. We come out of a past since we are at any moment of our lives the persons who have lived through and have been affected by a whole series of experiences which we recall only imperfectly at any given time. The most important "remembrance" of our past is to remember that we have come from God. He is our Source of being. He holds us in existence. His uncreated energies of love have surrounded us unceasingly all the days of our past life. As we grow in awareness of His all-ness in our lives, we will be able to look honestly at all of the past experiences, especially those that have hurt us and which we have conveniently repressed into our unconscious, afraid to look at them so as not to cause fresh hurts.

And yet, each moment remembered can be a blessing for growth or a curse that continues to hurt us, as Dr. Rollo May points out.[8] As in dying, so in healing of such memories, there are five stages: denial, anger, bargaining, depression and acceptance.[9] The more we grow in consciousness and prayer, the more we not only see the wounds inflicted by others and the effects of our own sins and recognize them as obstacles for us in our remembrance of God's loving presence, but the more we also are stirred by deeper faith and hope to believe that God can heal us. The desire to be healed and to surrender to God's transforming love becomes all-possessive. The recognition of the shadow-area within us is the first step in desiring an inner healing. Von Durkheim writes:

> It should be remembered that the ascent to the bright peaks of true being is always preceded by a descent into the dark depths, i.e. into those areas which have been thrust down

into the unconscious. It is only when we perceive and accept the Shadow, and painfully recognize our erroneous
responses to life; when we perceive, assimilate and live
through the figures which personify the repressed energies,
that the way towards true union with essential being is
opened and the new self, born from essence, becomes free
to grow.[10]

For a Christian, this healing of memories takes place
in three steps of prayer, sharing and faith-contact. The
first step is individual, inner prayer. The second is confession which achieves a particular power when it is in the
sacramental form of the Sacrament of Reconciliation. The
third is community whose deepest faith-source and most
powerful presence is the Eucharist.[11]

In such inner healings, we begin to experience already
the power of the Resurrection. The knowledge of where we
come from, both as past, from God and from the brokenness through the "ungodly" in our lives, becomes fused in
a present awareness of Jesus Christ living within us. This
brings us a constant state of our weakness, an inner crying
out for mercy and God's condescending love that the
Greek Fathers called "penthos."[12] It is also called *humility,* an infused state of knowledge that readily gives us a
perspective of truth as seen from God's point of view.

TRANSFORMING CONSCIOUSNESS

To the degree that the process of transformation takes
place in us, so also will the liberating, illuminating, kind-
ing spark of the Infinite Light shine more and more fre-
quently until finally it becomes a part of the basic part of
our daily life. The center and meaning of life will now no

longer be in persons or things outside of us or, above all, in our own selfish beings, but only in the Divine Trinity. We are consciously now living "according to the image and likeness" that is Jesus Christ. Jesus Christ is seen as an abiding light living within us and in all things around us. His light shines day and night within our hearts and in our intelligence. It bathes us in His radiance and knows no setting. It is living and life-giving, transforming into light those whom His light enlightens.

Such a gift of living in the light of God depends not on our human efforts to acquire. This is not to "see" God as light in a vision, in a visualized or intellectualized form of God as light. It comes to those who have embraced the crucified Lord. They have embraced true poverty of spirit, an adequate sense of their creatureliness that roots man in a "truthful" relationship with God and fellow-man. Only the Spirit can enlighten such Christians through an illumination to comprehend the incomprehensible. The Holy Spirit takes away the darkness from their minds and fills them with a heavenly light to understand the inner workings of the Trinity. The uncreated energies bathe them as the sun casts its warm rays upon the whole world. Such contemplatives truly "see" God everywhere, in all things.

For such purified contemplatives the Spirit reveals the Father at every moment, unceasingly begetting the Son within them. The Son is never separated from the Father nor from the Spirit of Love. Three Persons in one light, all distinct, yet none of them separated. The contemplative lives in that abiding experience of the inter-penetration of the Trinitarian Persons, their energies shining through every part of his or her being.

The energizing light of God's loving presence is seen not only within the contemplative but is seen bathing every creature outside in His glorious light. He is the Source of all life. He is energizing life. He gives life to everything that is. God's providence extends to every little detail in the universe just as the light of the sun shines everywhere. If we do not see Him in His all-pervasive, energizing presence, then we are blind and are not filled with His light. We are truly blind to that degree that we fail to see Him everywhere. The whole material world is the "locus" now for God's presence to come forth and be served by the contemplative in true, humble love. Although God is immovable, yet He is always seen by such a purified contemplative as movement. He fills all things, transcends all. He is immaterial, yet He pervades all matter.

He has no mouth to speak, yet He speaks His Word throughout all of creation. He has no hand to grasp man and guide him but man knows God touches Him with His divine hand in the touch of each human being. Into the eyes of every suffering human being such a contemplative looks and sees God's face. St. Symeon the New Theologian (+1022) best describes such an infused gift of seeing God as light everywhere:

> This shines brilliantly within me like a lamp,
> or rather that first is seen in the heavens,
> yes, which infinitely above the heavens in a very obscured way
> invisibly makes itself seen.
> But when I strive energetically and with force ask it to shine
> or better, to make itself more clearly to be seen from on high,
> it separates me from all things below and unites me
> with its unspeakable brilliance,
> or it suddenly shows itself completely within me,
> a spherical light, gentle and divine,

with form, with shape, in a formless form.
It is seen as much and speaks to me . . . [13]

HOW TO PRAY ALWAYS

Such a vision of God as permeating light, discovered by purified faith, hope and love, is exciting. We thrill at what awaits us, at what could be possible, if . . . Is such a consciousness a pure gift of God that He freely gives to some few whom He singles out with no respect for their efforts? Could we truly do anything to prepare ourselves for such a gift?

In Eastern Christianity the Augustinian problem of merit and grace, nature and supernature never arose. This was due primarily to the Eastern Christian theologians who theologized out of a prayerful experience of God's revelation found in Holy Scripture. In Scripture they found God as uncreated energies in all material things of this universe. They firmly believed that everything was gift from God. Yet they knew also that human beings had to want that gift. We human beings have not only to desire constantly to be pure of heart in order to see God everywhere but we have to cooperate with God's ever-present grace to become pure of heart by a constant dying to anything in our live that would prevent God's energies from transforming us into His loving children. God does give His gifts freely, yet He does expect us to cooperate with His graces.

The early Christians learned to pray always because they knew that was the command of Jesus Christ. That was truth; to live constantly in the awareness that God is always loving and is always present, communicating that love to His children. Therefore, simply it is not to be considered an extraordinary state given to a few chosen souls, but it is like the gift of life given to all who are now alive. It is a maturing of the potential in all of us and this God wishes to happen since He launches us into life in order that we may receive more abundantly the life that Jesus Christ came to give us.

Jesus Himself had taught them: "Then Jesus told them a parable about the need to pray continually and never lose heart" (Lk 18:1). St. Paul gave the same teaching common in the early Church: "never to cease praying" (1 Th 5:17). He knew that Christians should live for God and seek at all times to give Him glory. "Whatever you eat, whatever you drink, whatever you do at all, do it for the glory of God" (1 Co 10:31).

The first step, therefore, in praying always is to have a constant desire to live in the awareness of God's presence as love in every facet of our lives. Desire is the most primary act we can give God. It is the most primary place where the Holy Spirit begins the movement of us into deeper levels of consciousness of God's all-embracing, loving presence. If we freely turn away from such desiring because we desire lesser loves than that of God, then God will turn Himself away from us.

> I know all about you: how you are neither cold nor hot. I wish you were one or the other, but since you are neither, but only lukewarm, I will spit you out of my mouth. I am the one who reproves and disciplines all those he love: so repent in real earnest. Look, I am standing at the door, knocking. If one of you hears me calling and opens the door, I will come in to share his meal, side by side with him (Rv 3: 15-20).

Part of this effective desire is that we do all within our power to purify our minds and hearts from any self-attachment. We have already commented on the necessity of *praxis* or the whole ascetical life that embraces the negativity of removing from our lives all selfishness or sin and positively to live in union with Jesus Christ the Christian life of virtues, especially love towards all. But part of the *praxis* is also our efforts "to be present" to God as far as lies within our power. It consists in directing the power of our will to want to remain in constant remembrance of God's presence, by effectively wanting to obey His holy will in each moment.

But is it possible to think of God always? We must not confuse any individual, concentrated act of praying with the state or *habitus* of prayer. No human being can be engaged constantly in actual prayer, vocal or mental, as the Messalians of the early Church insisted on in pushing toward an unreal, heretical position.[14] Yet is it possible to bring such moments of conscious concentration upon God so that we are more or less in continuous thought of Him?

This, we must recognize easily enough from our own busy lives as practically impossible. Our duties demand other acts of concentration. God wants the housewife to be attentive as she prepares her meals. The truck driver should be conscientiously attentive to driving his truck. The teacher concentrates fully on preparing his or her classes and with full attention teaches the subject matter. Psychologically a mental derangement would be the result if one pushed his mental powers to such concentration on the spiritual world and removed himself from external occupations.

DOING THE WILL OF GOD

We have all been taught that it suffices to have a "virtual" intention to do all for God's glory and then everything we do, covered by such an enduring intention, would be pleasing to God. But remembering God's presence and seeking to please Him in all actions are more than that. In order to be totally obedient to God's will, expressed by His commands and wishes through delicate inspirations of the Holy Spirit, we must consciously turn within ourselves and seek to be in touch with God's inner communication. It is a centering in faith, hope and love upon God as our Ultimate Concern at all times. It is a striving to have a "pure heart" at all times so that we, in our consciousness, have God as the motivating force behind all of our actions.

St. Basil, one of the most practical and common-sensed of all the Saints in Christian history, described the essence of prayer as this continued remembrance of God and our desire to do all things to please Him:

> . . . so the Christian directs every action, small and great, according to the will of God, performing the action at the same time with care and exactitude, and keeping his thoughts fixed upon the One who gave him the work to do. In this way, he fulfills the saying, 'I set the Lord always in my sight; for He is at my right hand, that I be not moved' and he also observes the precept, 'Whether you eat or drink or whatsoever else you do, do all to the glory of God.' . . . We should perform every action as if under the eyes of the Lord and think every thought as if observed by Him . . . . fulfilling the words of the Lord: 'I seek not my own will but the will of Him that sent me, the Father.'[15]

Such a remembrance of God is a gift from God that is progressively given to those who desire it and strive to live according to the gift they have already received. It is rooted in faith, hope and love and can grow as we cooperate in each event of every day. It is to live in the "divine milieu," to use Teilhard de Chardin's phrase, that permeates, influences, guides and determines everything we do. But this is not a static concept, as has been already said in earlier chapters, that pictures God looking down upon us and waiting for us to make the right choices. He is a dynamic energizing force that permeates us and surrounds us. Our efforts must consist in putting ourselves within the orbit of God's loving presence and there working to do all things to please Him.

PRAISE AND THANKSGIVING

A true index as to the degree of our praying always comes in the quality and amount of praise and thanksgiving that permeates our daily living. If we believe in God's dynamic, loving presence at each moment, we can only praise Him for His love. We have new eyes to see each event in His love. We soon by God's grace develop a new way of viewing all things, since our faith tells us that *all* things work unto good for those who love the Lord (Rm 8: 28). With St. Paul we too can say through experience: "Be happy at all times; pray constantly; and for all things give thanks to God, because this is what God expects you to do in Christ Jesus" (1 Th 5:18).

We soon move into a spirit of constant adoration of God for His loving presence. His energizing love communicates itself in all things. Everything is a point of praising God, not only because of His gifts, but above all for His very own loving presence. The distinction between what is painful, a setback, a calamity and what is pleasant, a success and honor, disappears as we see through all events and creatures that touch our lives and see all things as "signs" of God's great love for us.

THE MODERN PROPHET

As we are purified of our own vision of reality and place ourselves by an ever increasing infusion from the Spirit of Jesus Christ of faith, hope and love, God pours into us His Word. We live to let Him have His way, His Word, in our lives. "Be it done unto me according to Thy Word" becomes for us our constant, prayerful act of surrender as Mary, the Mother of God, continually said her fiat of surrender (Lk 1:38). We too are called by God to live according to His interior law that He wishes to write upon our hearts (Jr 31:33). Each Christian is called by God through Baptism to be a prophet, collaborating with the word of God in mediating the saving, healing word to others in the context of his life's activities. The Christian contemplative goes out into the world of action with an interior knowledge because of his or her intimate relationship with God. This penetrates every thought, word and deed as the contemplative lives out that Word interiorized and experienced through a constant listening within. Surrendering to God's uncreated energies, such a modern prophet begins to experience unsuspected areas of creativity. His actions are now one with the movement of the Creator. He puts himself totally at the disposition of the divine energies. He gains such spiritual gifts as divine sight, divine hearing, the ability to read the hearts of other people. Above all, he develops the greatest in the area of love for the whole human race and for every creature alive and sustained by God's loving presence. He seeks to serve and draw out the best hidden in each being whom he meets.

This loving power is God's very own life, transforming the world into light and heat, the light that allows each human being to "see" God, loving us human beings in each situation and the heat to warm our human hearts to adore the almighty, tender loving God as we lovingly open ourselves to love one another. The love of God pours into us, allowing us to see the power of the Spirit of Jesus Christ working in the lives of all human beings, regardless of whatever culture or religion. We breathe more freely as we live on higher plateaus that stretch out into infinity. The walls and ghettoes that our fearful, anxious selves have constructed because we were living in darkness and ignorance and did not realize God was present in all things, these come crashing down.

We stretch out our empty hands and humbly ask God to fill them with His energies of love. We beg Him to use our weaknesses in order that His glory, His *Shekinah,* may appear in each event. We cry out in pain that the full Jesus Christ be brought forth in glory. We offer our hands and lips to be channels of the healing power of Jesus Christ among His people again. Praying incessantly is now, not so much saying prayers, but a living in a constant con-sciousness of God's beauty, found "inside" of all matter. We humbly take off our shoes, all our human securities, and in mute adoration we surrender in loving submission. Surrender is true freedom and freedom is the joy of the children of God who have already entered into a sharing in the Kingdom of Heaven. Truly, the world of matter has been the place where God has diaphanously shone forth. God is at the heart of matter. And matter is moving, by our prayerful contemplation of God and man in loving ser-vice, towards spirit. The world that is groaning in its limitations of matter is slowly emerging as a transfigured Heavenly Jerusalem.

Then I saw a new heaven and a new earth; the first heaven and the first earth had disappeared now, and there was no longer any sea. I saw the holy city, and the new Jerusalem, coming down from God out of heaven, as beautiful as a bride all dressed for her husband. Then I heard a loud voice call from the throne, 'You see this city? Here God lives among men. He will make his home among them; they shall be his people, and he will be their God; his name is God-with-them. He will wipe away all tears from their eyes; there will be no more death, and no more mourning or sadness The world of the past has gone.'

Then the One sitting on the throne spoke: 'Now I am making the whole of creation new' he said. 'Write this: that what I am saying is sure and will come true.' And then he said, 'It is already done. I am the Alpha and the Omega, the Beginning and the End. I will give water from the well of life free to anybody who is thirsty; it is the rightful inheritance of the one who proves victorious; and I will be his God and he a son to me (Rv 21: 1-7).

OH, GOD!

I sit in early morn
and gaze on my God.
I see the light of His smile
in the soft rays of the dawn
that tip-toe into my room.
His light covers me
and warms me.
I stir to His presence
  around me,
    within me.

The cocoon that so many years
of silent births and deaths
spun into a prison
begins to split down its sides.
Slowly His loving energies
pour over me.
I stretch toward Life.
I move toward Light
from out my hibernating darkness.

Oh, God! You gave me wings!
They unfold, wet and packed-tight,
to spangled colors of rainbow fair.
God, was all this beauty and power
always there, locked inside?
Were You always present,
warm Light of piercing Love?
Why so long to be called to life?
Why so much prison cell confining?
Where were You, God?

Son, know that My Love is eternal.
My presence can never become absence.
My Light can never turn to darkness.
My Spring is never winter.
I have always encompassed you
with My energies of Love.
I live within you.
I am the Force around you.
You can never be outside
of My Uncreated Love.

But it is you
who in womb-tomb
had to open up to My Life.
You had to want
  Light over darkness,
  Life over death,
  Love over fear.

In due time I sent
  My spring-warmth into your life.
I laughed through their eyes.
I encircled you in their arms.
I breathed My Life in their breath
and you came forth in love.

Oh, God!
Let Your energies bathe me today.
May Your light encompass me.
Fill me with Your loving presence.
Send me Your love again,
that I may stretch
my colored wings
  out and up
  and fly in ecstasy
  dizzily up into the heavens,
  leaving the bonds of this earth,
behind in remembrance of what was.

Oh, God!
Be Spring again.
Let Winter finish,
ne'er to return.
Let only Your Love
reign supreme.
Bring me again Your Life!

George A. Maloney, S.J.

FOOTNOTES

Introduction

[1] Kahlil Gibran: "God," in: *The Madman* (N.Y.: A.A. Knopf, 1965) pp 9-10.

[2] G. M. Hopkins: "Hurrahing in Harvest," in: *A Hopkins Reader,* ed. John Pick (N.Y.-London: Oxford Univ. Press, 1953) p. 15.

[3] Cited by Maria F. Mahoney: *The Meaning in Dreams and Dreaming* (Secaucus, N.J.: The Citadel Press, 1976) p. 138.

[4] These ideas are more fully developed in: *Woman Is the Glory of Man,* by E. Danniel and B. Olivier (Westminster, Md.: Newman Press, 1966).

[5] Quoted by Geoffrey Grigson: *G. M. Hopkins* (London: Longmans, Green & Co., 1955) p. 22.

[6] G. M. Hopkins: "A Vision of the Mermaids."

Chapter 1

[1] M. Rokeach: *The Open and Closed Mind* (N.Y.: Basic Boks, 1960); E. Chesen: *Religion May Be Hazardous To Your Health* (N.Y.: Collier Books, 1972).

[2] C. Jung: *Psychology and Religion* (New Haven, Conn.: Yale Univ. Press, 1938).

[3] A.J. Heschel: *Man Is Not Alone* (N.Y.: Farrar, Straus and Giroux, 1951) p. 36.

[4] C. A. Van Peursen: *Body, Soul, Spirit: A Survey of the Body-Mind Problem* (London: Oxford Univ. Press, 1966) p. 35.

[5] Cf.: Karl Rahner: *On the Theology of Death* (N.Y.: Sheed & Ward, 1961) pp. 21-39; Paul Chauchard: *Man and Cosmos* (N.Y.: 1965), tr. G. Courtright, p. 143; Jose-Maria Gonzalez-Ruiz: "Should We De-Mythologize the 'Separated Soul?'," in: *Concilium;* Vol. 41, *Dogma,*

the Problem of Eschatology (N.Y.: Glen Rock; N.J.: Paulist Press, 1969) pp. 82-96; Anton Grabner-Haider: "The Biblical Understanding of 'Resurrection' and 'Glorification,' " *Ibid.,* pp. 66-81.

[6] For a thorough presentation of this concept and related terms in both the Old and the New Testaments, cf.: John L. McKenzie: *Dictionary of the Bible* (Milwaukee: Bruce Publishing Co., 1965) pp. 840-845.

[7] Cf.: C.A. Van Peursen: *op. cit.,* p. 96.

[8] *Ibid.,* pp. 97-98.

[9] Cf.: Emil Brunner: *Man in Revolt* (London: Lutterworth Press, 1953) pp. 97-98.

[10] OIn the problem of nature and supernature cf.: H. de Lubac, S.J.: *Surnaturel* (Paris, 1946) and G.A. Maloney, S.J.: *Man—The Divine Icon* (Pecos, N.M.: Dove Publication, 1973) pp. 15-20.

[11] Pierre Teilhard de Chardin: *The Divine Milieu* (N.Y.: Harper & Bros., 1960), ed. Bernard Wall, p. 110.

[12] Cf.: M. Heidegger: *Plato's Doctrine of Truth,* tr. John Barlow, in: *Philosophy in the Twentieth Century,* ed. Wm. Barrett and H.D. Aiken (N.Y.: Random, 1962).

[13] *The Divine Milieu, op. cit.,* p. 127.

[14] Cf.: G. Maloney, S.J.: *The Cosmic Christ. From Paul to Teilhard* (N.Y.: Sheed and Ward, 1968).

[15] P. Teilhard de Chardin, *op. cit.,* p. 35.

Chapter 2

[1] E. S. Gaustad: *Dissent in American Religion* (Chicago: 1973) p. 149.

[2] Gaustad, *op. cit.,* pp. 150-151.

[3] V. E. Frankl: *La psychotherapie et son image de l'homme* (Paris, 1970) p. 150.

4 Dr. Louis Dupré: "Transcendence and Immanence as Theological Categories," in: *Proceedings of the Thirty-First Annual Convention of the Catholic Theological Society of America;* Vol. 31, 1976, pp. 5.

5 St. Gregory of Nyssa: *Song of Songs; PG* 44, 1000 D, quoted from *From Glory to Glory*, ed. by J. Danielou and H. Musurillo (N.Y.: Scribner, 1961) p. 247.

6 Pseudo-Dionysius: *Mystical Theology* in: *Dionysius the Areopagite. The Divine Names and the Mystical Theology,* tr. C. E. Rolt (London, SPCK, 1920) p. 191.

7 Archbishop Joseph Raya: *The Face of God* (Denville, N.J.: Dimension Books, 1976) pp. 37-38.

8 Cf.: G. Maloney, S.J.: *A Theology of Uncreated Energies* (Milwaukee: Marquette Univ. Press, 1978) ch. 3, pp. 60-98.

9 G. M. Hopkins: "Hurrahing in Harvest," op. cit., p. 15.

10 St. Gregory of Nyssa: *Christian Mode of Life,* in: *The Fathers of the Church* (Wash. D.C., 1967) Vol. 58, p. 130.

11 *Gregoire Palamas—Les Triads pour la defense des Saints Hesychastes,* 3 vols., ed. by John Meyendorff (Louvain: Spicilegium Sacrum Lovaniense, 1959) Triads II, 2, 9.

12 G. M. Hopkins: "God's Grandeur," op. cit., p. 13.

13 Pierre Teilhard de Chardin: *The Divine Milieu* (N.Y.: Harper & Bros., 1960) p. 111.

14 A. J. Heschel: *God in Search of Man* (N.Y.: Farrar, Straus and Giroux, 1955) p. 39.

15 Thomas Merton: *Contemplation in a World of Action* (Garden City, N.Y.: Doubleday, 1971) p. 54.

Chapter 3

1 M. Kelsey: *The Other Side of Silence* (N.Y.—Paramus, N.J.: Paulist Press, 1976), especially pp. 178 ff.

[2] *Ibid.*, pp. 178-179.

[3] Quoted by Maria F. Mahoney: *The Meaning in Dreams and Dreaming* (Secaucus, N.J.: The Citadel Press, 1976) p. 13.

[4] Maria Mahoney, *op. cit.,* pp. 26-27.

[5] His workshop has been developed into a book: *At a Journal Workshop. The basic text and guide for using the Intensive Journal* (N.Y.: Dialogue House Library, 1975), especially pp. 228 ff. Morton Kelsey has written on this same subject from a Christian viewpoint: *God, Dreams and Revelation* (Minneapolis: Augsburg Publishing House, 1974) and *Dreams: The Dark Speech of the Spirit* (Garden City, N.Y.: Doubleday and Company, Inc., 1968).

[6] St. John of the Cross: *The Ascent of Mount Carmel,* Bk. 2, ch. 13, in *The Collected Works of St. John of the Cross,* tr. Kieran Kavanaugh, O.C.D. and Otilio Rodriguez, O.C.D. (Wash. D.C.: ICS Publications, Institute of Carmelite Studies, 1973) pp. 140-141.

[7] Thomas Merton: *The Climate of Monastic Prayer* (Spencer, Mass.: Cistercian Publications, 1968) p. 128.

[8] Thomas Merton, *op. cit.,* p. 147.

[9] Cf.: Leonard Boase, S.J.: *The Prayer of Faith* (St. Louis: B. Herder Book Co., 1962).

[10] On the theological presentation of St. Maximus' system of contemplating the Logos in the world, see the excellent work of Lars Thunberg: *Microcosm and Mediator. The Theological Anthropology of Maximus Confessor* (Copenhagen-Lund, 1965), also A. Riou: *Le monde et l'eglise selon Maxime le confesseur* (Paris: Beauchesne, 1973) and Hans Urs von Balthasar: *Kosmische Liturgie* (Einsiedeln, 1961).

[11] Cf.: Riou, *op. cit.,* p. 28.

[12] Thunberg: *op. cit.,* pp. 77-78.

[13] St. Maximus: *The Earlier Ambiqua,* tr. Polycarp Sherwood, O.S.B. (Rome: Herder, 1955) pp. 170-171.

[14] St. Maximus: *Ambigua; PG* XCI, 1081 C.

[15] St. Maximus: *The Four Centuries on Charity,* Bk. I, 95, tr. Polycarp Sherwood, O.S.B., in: *Ancient Christian Writers,* Vol. XXI (Westminster, Md., Newman, 1955) p. 151.

[16] St. Maximus: *Relation Motionis; PG* XC, 124 A.

Chapter 5

[1] An excellent new work on this subject is: James R. Roberts: *The Body/Soul Metaphor in the Papal/Imperial Polemic on Eleventh Century Church Reform,* (unpublished Master of Arts Thesis at the University of British Columbia, 1977).

[2] G. Murray: *Five Stages of Greek Religion* (Garden City, N.Y.: Doubleday and Co., no date) p. 154.

[3] Cf. Sidney Hook: *The Quest for Being* (N.Y.: Delta Books, 1963) p. 73 ff.

[4] *Letter to Diognetus,* cited by Roland H. Bainton: *Early Christianity* (N.Y.: D. Van Nostrand Co., Inc., 1960) p. 153.

[5] Rosemary R. Reuther: *Religion and Sexism* (N.Y.: Simon and Schuster, 1974) p. 153.

[6] R. O'Connell, S.J.: "Body and Soul," in: *The Way* (London, Jan., 1970) pp. 12, 16, 17.

[7] St. Augustine: *Marriage and Concupiscence,* I, 15, 17, CSEL (Vienna) 42, pp. 229-230, cited by J. Noonan, Jr.: *Contraception* (Cambridge, Mass.: Harvard Univ. Press, 1965) p. 137.

[8] D. H. Lawrence: *The Rainbow* (N.Y.: The Viking Press, 1961) p .54.

[9] K. Gibran: *The Prophet, op. cit.,* pp. 15-16.

[10] Cf.: my work on this theme: *The Cosmic Christ—from Paul to Teilhard* (N.Y.: Sheed and Ward, 1968).

[11] Frank Gilroy: The Subject Was Roses.

[12] *Constitution on the Church* in Vatican Council II. The Conciliar and Post-Conciliar Documents ed. A. Flannery, O.P. (Northport, N.Y.: Costello Publishing Co., 1975) II 32, p. 389.

[13] *Ibid.,* II 33, p. 391.

Chapter 4

[1] John G. Neihardt: *Black Elk Speaks* (Lincoln, Neb.: Univ. of Nebraska Press, 1961).

[2] *Ibid.,* pp. 198-200.

[3] *Ibid.,* pp. 42-43.

[4] Cf.: "Ecosystems and Systematics," in *Theology Today,* XXIX, no. 4 (1972), p. 113.

[5] *De Ecclesia* (Wash. D.C.: *National Catholic Welfare Conference,* 1964) p. 3.

[6] *The Divine Milieu, op. cit.,* p. 31.

[7] Pierre Cren: "The Christian and the World According to Teilhard de Chardin," in *Concilium,* Vol. XIX (N.Y.; Paramus, N.J.: Paulist Press, 1966) p. 42.

[8] G. A. Maloney, S.J.: *The Cosmic Christ from Paul to Teilhard* (N.Y.: Sheed & Ward, 1968), esp. pp. 182-220.

[9] Alfons Auer: "The Changing Character of the Christian Understanding of the World," in: *The Christian and the World* (N.Y.: P. J. Kenedy & Sons, 1965) p. 32.

[10] E. Schillebeeckx, ed.,: *The Church and Mankind,* in: *Concilium,* Vol. 1 N.Y.: Paulist Press, 1964) pp. 81-82.

[11] *The Divine Milieu, op. cit.,* p. 135.

[12] Teilhard: "Super-humanité, super-Christ, super-charité," in: *Oeuvres de Pierre de Chardin,* Vol. 9 (Paris: Seuil, 1965) pp. 213-217.

[13] K. Gibran: *The Prophet* (N.Y.: Alfred A. Knopf Publisher, 1963) p. 27.

[14] T.S. Eliot: *Four Quartets* (New York: Harcourt & Brace and Co., 1943) p. 39.

Chapter 6

[1] For three Catholic theologians who hold a similar view, cf.: Hans Kung: *On Being a Christian* (N.Y.: Doubleday, 1976); Piet Schoonenberg, S.J.: *The Christ* (N.Y.: Herder & Herder, 1971); and Jon Sobrino, S.J.: *Christology at the Crossroads* (Maryknoll, N.Y.: Orbis Books, 1978).

[2] Cf.: Louis Bouyer: *Eucharist* (Notre Dame, Ind.: Univ. of Notre Dame Press, 1968) p. 467.

[3] *Didache,* 9, tr. Henry Bettinson in *Documents of the Christian Church* (London, 1959) p. 90.

[4] Monika K. Hellwig: *The Eucharist and the Hunger of the World* (N.Y.—Paramus, N.J.: Paulist Press/Deus Book, 1976) p. 42.

[5] Cf.: Max Thurian: *The Eucharistic Memorial* (Richmond, Va.: John Knox Press, 1960-61), the whole first chapter.

[6] Teilhard de Chardin: *Hymn of the Universe* (N.Y.: Harper & Row, 1965) p. 92.

[7] Cf.: P.C. Hodgson: *Jesus—Word and Presence* (Phil. Pa.: Fortress Press, 1971) pp. 220-291.

[8] Cf.: #10: Constitution on the Liturgy of Vatican Council II.

[9] Max Delespesse: *Church Community Leaven and Life-Style* (Ottawa, 1969) p. 30.

[10] Monika Hellwig, *op. cit.,* p. 50.

[11] Teilhard de Chardin: *The Divine Milieu, op. cit.,* pp. 104-105.

Chapter 7

[1] St. John Chrysostom: Commentary on Ps. 133: *PG* 55:386.

[2] G. Maloney, S.J.: *Inward Stillness,* (Denville, N.J.: Dimension Bks., 1976) p. 122.

[3] Libellus Jordani de Saxonia, no. 12 in: *Monumenta Historica S. Patris Nostri Dominici,* fasc. II (Rome, 1935).

[4] Cf.: M. Jacob: *Théologie de l'Ancien Testament,* (Paris: Neuchatel, 1956) p. 41.

[5] Louis Lochet, S.J.: "Apostolic Prayer" in: *Finding God in All Things.* Essays in Ignatian Spirituality selected from *Christus,* tr. by William J. Young, S.J. (Chicago: H. Regnery Co., 1958) p. 175.

[6] St. John of the Cross: *The Ascent of Mount Carmel,* Bk. II, 3, in: The Collected Works of St. John of the Cross, tr. by Kieran Kavanaugh, O.C.D. and Otilio Rodriguez, O.C.D. (Wash. D.C.: ICS Publications, 1973) pp. 121-122.

[7] Leonard Boase, S.J.: *The Prayer of Faith,* (St. Louis: B. Herder Book Co., 1962) p. 93.

[8] St. Symeon the New Theologian: *Catecheses,* ed. by B. Krivocheine in: *Sources Chrétiénnes Series* (Paris: Cerf, 1964) Vol. 104, no. 8, 57-67, p. 90.

[9] G. M. Hopkins: "As Kingfishers Catch Fire," op. cit., p. 19.

Chapter 8

[1] Carlos Castaneda: *Journey to Ixtlan* (N.Y.: Simon & Schuster, 1972) p. 299.

[2] R. Otto: *The Idea of the Holy* (N.Y.: Oxford Univ. Press, 1958) tr. J. W. Harvey, pp. 5-11.

[3] Carl Jung: *Collected Works* (Princeton, N.J.: Princeton Univ. Press, 1970) Vol. VIII, p. 217.

⁴ Peter Fransen, S.J.: *The New Life of Grace* (Brussels, Belgium: Desclee Co., 1969) pp. 312-313.

⁵ Three excellent works by J. M. Dechanet, O.S.B. may help a Christian to understand how important yoga can be for aiding the Christian toward deeper prayer: *Christian Yoga; Yoga in Ten Lessons;* and *Yoga and God: An Invitation to Christian Yoga.*

⁶ Karlfried Graf von Durckheim: *The Way of Transformation* (London, 1971) p. 61.

⁷ Thomas Merton: *Seeds of Contemplation* (Norfolk: Dell Books 1949) p. 59.

⁸ Rollo May: *The Art of Counseling* (Nashville: Abingdon Press, 1967) p. 35.

⁹ For an excellent development of this theme, see: Dennis and Matthew Linn: *Healing Life's Hurts: Healing Memories Through the Five Stages of Forgiveness* (N.Y./Ramsey, N.J.: Paulist Press, 1978) pp. 87-179.

¹⁰ *Op. cit.,* p. 74.

¹¹ D. and M. Linn, *op. cit.,* pp. 180-191. Cf. also the excellent article by Fr. Francis Martin: "The Healing of Memories," in: *Review For Religious* (May, 1973) pp. 498-507.

¹² On this theme, see my book: *Inward Stillness* (Denville, N.J.: Dimension Books, 1976) pp. 105-120.

¹³ St. Symeon the New Theologian: *Hymns of Divine Love,* tr. G. A. Maloney, S.J. (Denville, N.J.: Dimension Bks., 1975) Hymn 50, p. 251.

¹⁴ Cf.: I Hausherr, S.J.: "Comment Priaient les Pères," in: *Revue d'Ascetique et de Mystique* (Jan.-March, 1956).

¹⁵ St. Basil: *Regulae Fusius; PG* 920 C-921 B, *Regula 5.*